2

(1) 40 cm in diameter Instructions on Page 59
(2) 36 cm in diameter Instructions on Page 60

Gorgeous Pineapple Doilies

(3) 33 cm in diameter   Instructions on Page 61
(4) 28 cm in diameter   Instructions on Page 62

5

6

Gorgeous Pineapple Doilies

(5) 32 cm in diameter   Instructions on Page 63
(6) 33 cm in diameter   Instructions on Page 64

6

Gorgeous Pineapple Doilies

(7) 40 cm in diameter   Instructions on Page 65
(8) 38 cm in diameter   Instructions on Page 66

Lovely Small Doilies Crocheted with only 10g

12

You'll need:
Crochet cotton DMC No. 40, 10g Pink (104)
Steel crochet hook:
Crochet hook No. I
Finished size:
25 cm in diameter

Making instructions:
Make a loop at the end of the cotton. **Row 1:** Ch-3, 1-dc, ch-3 (2-dc at a time, ch-3) 8 times in ring. **Rows 2 – 13:** Referring to the chart, work pineapple patterns from Row 4. Make small pineapples from Row 6. **Rows 14 – 17:** Work 3-dc puff to make small flowers on top of pineapples. **Rows 18 – 20:** Work 68 net st. Of ch-5. **Row 21:** Repeat ch-3, 5-ch-p (sl st at the end p), ch-3 around.

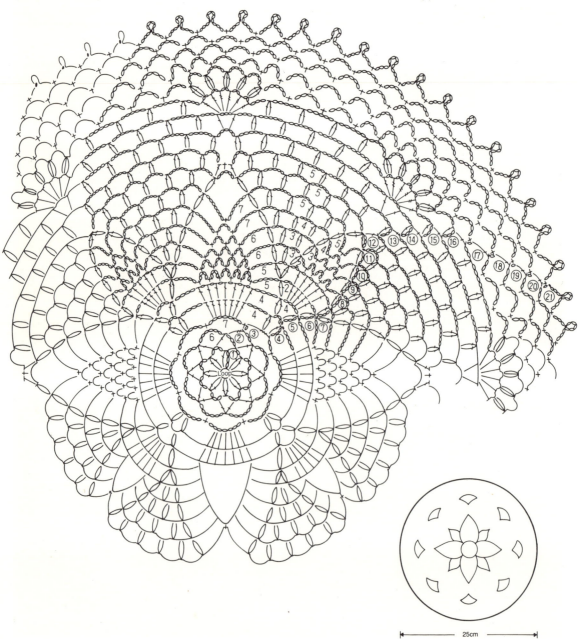

25cm

13

You'll need:
Crochet cotton DMC No. 40, 10g White (801)
Steel crochet hook:
Crochet hook No. I
Finished size:
22 cm in diameter
Making instructions:
Ch-8, sl st in 1st ch to form ring. **Row 1:** Ch-3 (1-dc, ch-1) 15 times in ring, sl st in 3rd st of beginning ch. **Row 2:** Ch-6 (1-dc, ch-3) to make 16 square meshes. **Row 3:** Ch-8 (1-dc, ch-5) to make 16 square meshes. **Row 4:** Ch-3, 2-dc, ch-5

(3-dc, ch-5) twice in each square mesh around (32 loops). **Row 5:** Work 32 net st of ch-5. **Row 6 – 8:** Referring to chart, repeat dc and ch. Cut thread off. **Row 9:** Start a new thread. Work '3-dc at a time in 1 square mesh on previous row twice and make ch-5 to join' 4 times. **Rows 10 – 15:** Make pineapple patterns with net st (1-sc, ch-5). Decrease the number of loops one by one. Work mesh between patterns by making 8 square meshes, increasing sts of ch from 1 to 5 sts. **Row 16:** Work 1-dc every 3-chs and make ch-p and shown in the chart to create scallop shape.

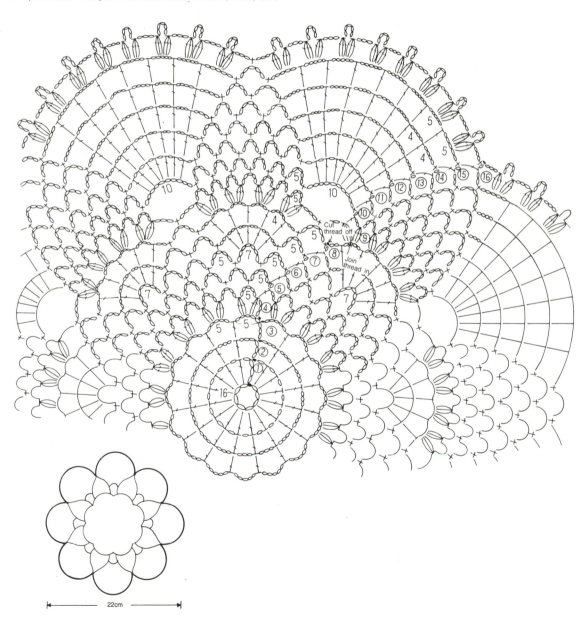

22cm

Doily Variations Crocheted with Only 10g

(15) 42 cm in diameter　(16) 24 cm in diameter　Instruction on Page 16, 17

15

16

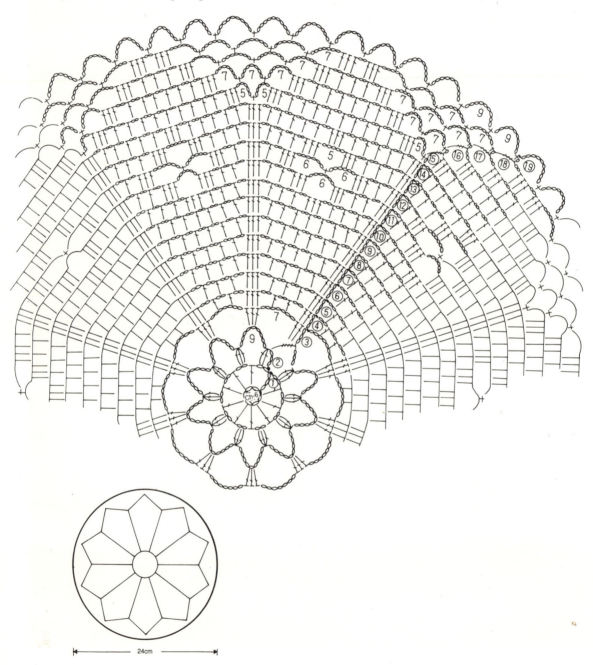

You'll need:
Crochet cotton DMC No. 40, 10g White (801)
Steel crochet hook:
Crochet hook No. I
Finished size:
24 cm in diameter
Making instructions:
Ch-6, sl st in 1st ch to form ring. **Row 1:** Ch-3, (1-dc, ch-2) 9 times in ring, sl st in 3rd st of beginning ch. **Row 2:** As shown, ch-3, 2-dc-puff, ch-9, (3-dc-puff, ch-9) 9 times. **Row 3:** Ch-3, 2-dc in ch-9 on previous row, ch-7, (3-dc in the next loop of ch-9, ch-7) to make 10 patterns in one round. **Rows 4 – 14:** As shown, ch-3, 2-dc, ch-2, repeat (3-dc, ch-2) around increasing 1 square mesh each on both sides of ch-3. From Row 10, work diaper patterns. **Rows 15 – 18:** Starting from the center of 3-dc, work ch, decreasing 1 square mesh each. **Row 19:** Work ch-9 around.

24cm

15

You'll need:

Crochet cotton DMC No. 40, 40g White (801)

Steel crochet hook:

Crochet hook No. I

Finished size:

42 cm in diameter

Making instructions:

Refer to 16 for instructions up to Row 19. **Row 19:** End with ch-4, 1-dtr instead of the last ch-9 as shown. **Row 20:** Work net st (1-sc, ch-9) around. **Row 21:** Ch-11, (1-dc, ch-8) in each loop of ch-9 on previous row. **Row 22:** Ch-5, (1-dc, ch-3). Work dc into ch to make 180 square meshes. **Rows 23 – 25:** Work 20 diaper patterns around. The number of chains changes in each row. **Rows 34, 35:** Ch-9 (1-dc, ch-6), sl st in 4th st of beginning ch to make 100 square meshes. **Rows 36 – 38:** 1 pattern will be created on two square meshes. There are 50 patterns around.

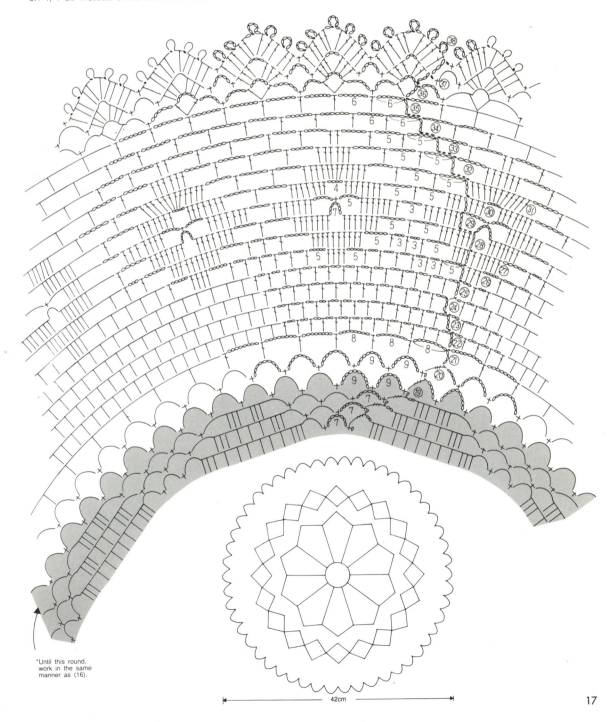

*Until this round, work in the same manner as (16).

42cm

17

Doily Variations Crocheted with Only 10g

(17) 38 cm in diameter   (18) 24 cm in diameter   Instructions on Page 20, 21

18

You'll need:
Crochet cotton DMC No. 40, 10g White (801)
Steel crochet hook:
Crochet hook No. I
Finished size:
24 cm in diameter
Making instructions:
First, make outside motif. Ch-10, sl st in 1st ch to form a ring. **Row 1:** Ch-3, 23-dc in ring, sl st in 3rd st of beginning ch. **Row 2:** Work net st (1-sc, ch-5) in every other dc on previous row to make 12 loops around. Make 24 pieces in the same way, however, from the second motif, join 2 loops together (3 loops inside and 5 loops outside should be left) to form doughnut shapes as shown. As for the central part,

ch-10, sl st in 1st ch to form ring. Work 12 net st (1-sc, 10-ch) in a ring with 1-dc instead of the last ch-5. **Row 2:** Ch-1, work net st (1-sc, ch-5) to make 12 loops. **Row 3:** Ch-8, (1-tr, ch-3, 1-dc) to make Y shape in each loop of the net st on previous row. Refer to P.45. **Rows 4 – 6:** Ch-1, work 24 net st (1-sc, ch-5). **Row 7:** Work Y shape pattern st of dtr in the same way as in Row 3. **Rows 8 – 11:** Ch-1, work 48 net sts. **Row 12:** In every loop of net sts on the previous row, work (1 tr, ch-3, 1-sc to join to the central loop of 3 loops inside a motif, ch-3, 1-tr to return to a loop on Row 11, ch-3, 1-sc, ch-3) 24 times. Cut thread off. As for edging, ch-3, 1-dc, ch-3. Work Y shape pattern st in 3 of 5 outside loops of the net st of a motif. Work 2-dc at a time in both sides of a motif.

24cm

17

You'll need:
Crochet cotton DMC No. 40, 30g White (801)
Steel crochet hook:
Crochet hook No. I
Finished size:
38 cm in diameter
Making instructions:
Row 1: Continue working on doily (18). To make the start easier, join the thread on the loop following the right one.

Rows 2 – 10: Work 1-dc, ch-3, 1-dc in each Y shape pattern st on Row 1. As row progresses, the number of chs between 1-dc, ch-3, 1-dc increases. Row 11: Increase 1st of ch between dc to 4 and 5 sts. Row 12: Ch-1, 1-sc, work 7-dc in ch-4 on the previous row, and 1-sc in ch-5. Make 72 pine tree pattern sts. Row 13: Ch-5, (1-tr, 1-ch) 7 times in every other pine tree pattern st on the previous row. Work 1-sc between pine tree pattern sts. Row 14: Ch-1. Work 1-sc, ch-p of ch-3 in ch on the previous row.

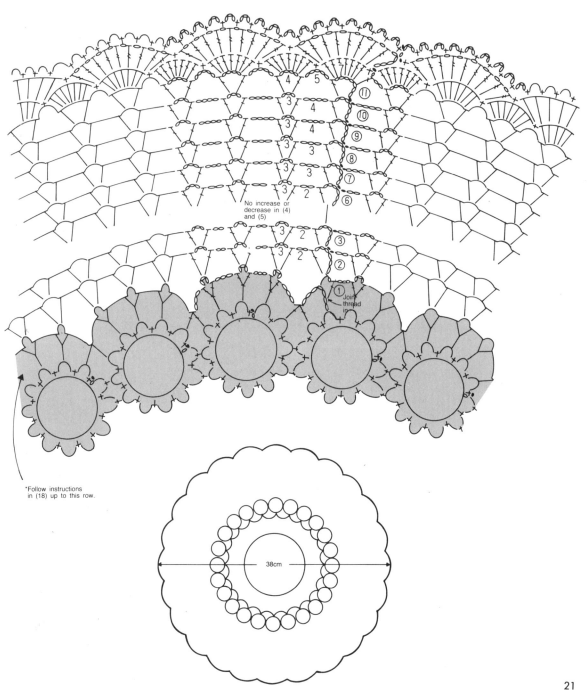

No increase or decrease in (4) and (5)

Join thread in

*Follow instructions in (18) up to this row.

38cm

Doily Variations Crocheted with Only 10g

(19) 25 cm in diameter

(21) 24 cm in diameter

22 (20) 33 cm in diameter Instructions on Page 70, 71

(22) 30 cm in diameter

Instructions on Page 24, 25

21

22

You'll need:
Crochet cotton DMC No. 40, 10g Light blue (361)
Steel crochet hook:
Crochet hook No. I
Finished size:
24 cm in diameter
Making instructions:
Ch-12, sl st in 1st ch to form a ring. **Row 1:** Ch-1 work 24-sc,

sl st in the beg. ch. **Rows 2 – 4:** Work 12 net sts, increasing sts of ch to 4 and 5 in Rows 3 and 4 respectively. **Row 5:** Work ch-5, 1-dc, ch-3, 1-dc, (1-dc, ch-2, 1-dc) each in 12 loops of net st with ch-3 between patterns to make 12 patterns. **Rows 6 – 17:** Work large and small flower patterns with dc and ch as shown. **Rows 18 – 19:** Work 48 loops of net set of ch-8. Work sc in ch sts. **Row 20:** Ch-1, 1-sc, ch-4, (1-p of ch-5, ch-4) 47 times.

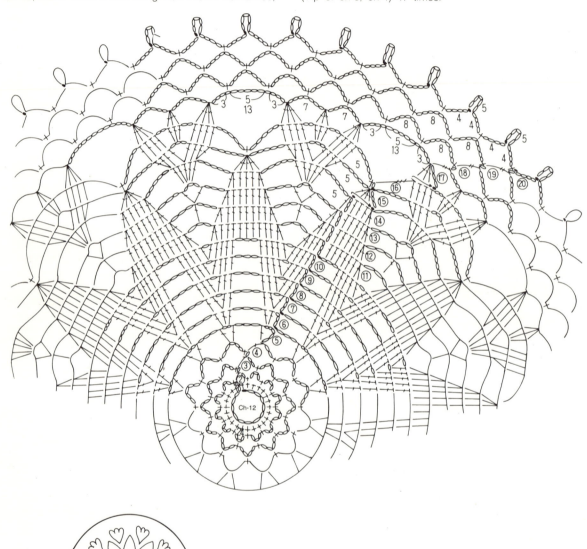

|← 24cm →|

You'll need:
Crochet cotton DMC No. 40, 20g White (801)
Steel crochet hook:
Crochet hook No. I
Finished size:
30 cm in diameter

Making instructions:
Follow instructions in Doily (21) up to row 19. **Rows 20 – 22:**
Work 48 net sts of ch-8. **Row 23:** Ch-8, (1-dc, ch-5, 1-dc) in
each loop of net sts on the previous row. Ch-5, 1-sc to join
to the next loop, ch-5, and repeat '1-dc, ch-5, 1-dc' in the
next loop to make 24 patterns. **Rows 24 – 26:** Work 24 small
flower patterns with dc and ch as shown. **Row 27:** Repeat
[Ch-5, 5-ch-p (sl st at the end p), ch-5] to make 72 patterns.

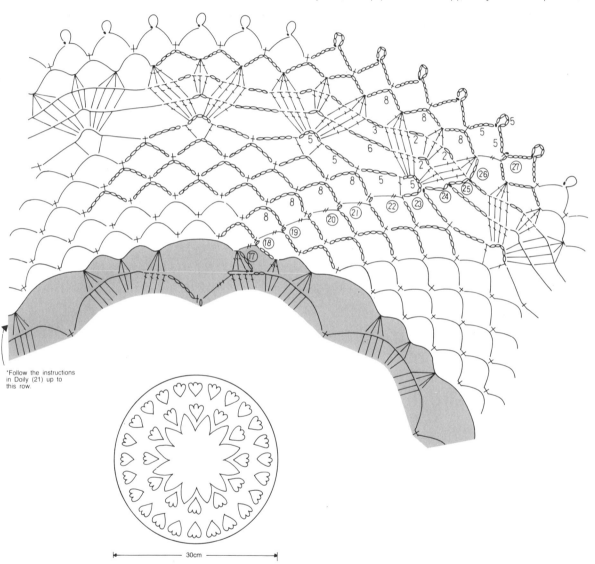

*Follow the instructions
in Doily (21) up to
this row.

30cm

Handkerchief Borders

(23), (24), (25) Instructions on Page 73   (28), (29), (30), (31) Instructions on Page 74

     (26), (27), (32) Instructions on Page 75

28

29

30

32

31

27

33

You'll need:
Crochet cotton DMC No. 40, 130g White (801) White hemp cloth 80 cm by 80 cm. 1 skein of embroidery thread No. 25 white.

Steel crochet hook:
Crochet hook No. I
Embroidery needle

Finished size:
108 cm in diameter

Making instructions:
Copy a design on a set position of the cloth. Embroider small flowers with double threads. **Row 1:** Ch-1, 1-sc around the cloth. **Row 2:** Work 200 loops of net sts of ch-5. **Rows 3 – 7:** Repeat (2-dc at a time, ch-3, 2-dc at a time) with ch-3 between patterns. **Rows 19 – 25:** Work fan-shape patterns. On Row 25, work 3-dc puff instead of fan-shape patterns. **Row 26:** Work inversed Y shape pattern st. **Rows 27 – 33:** Work net st of ch-7 on Row 27. Work in the same manner as in Rows 3 – 7 until Row 32 increasing sts of ch. On the last row, work sl st in the 1st chain of previous ch-3 to make zigzag patterns.

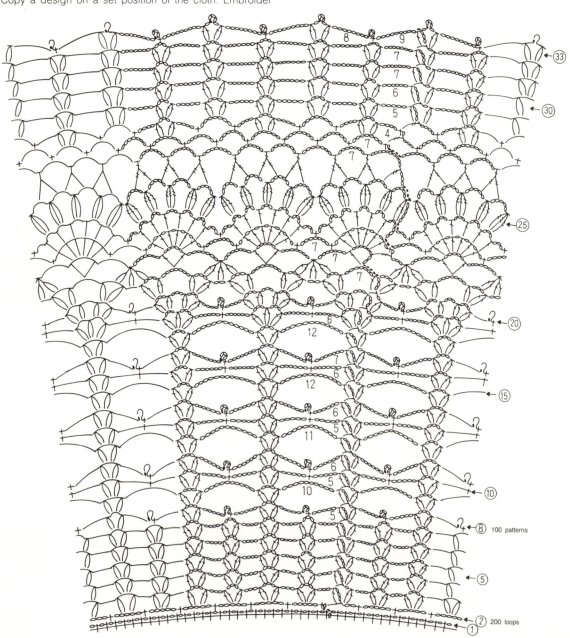

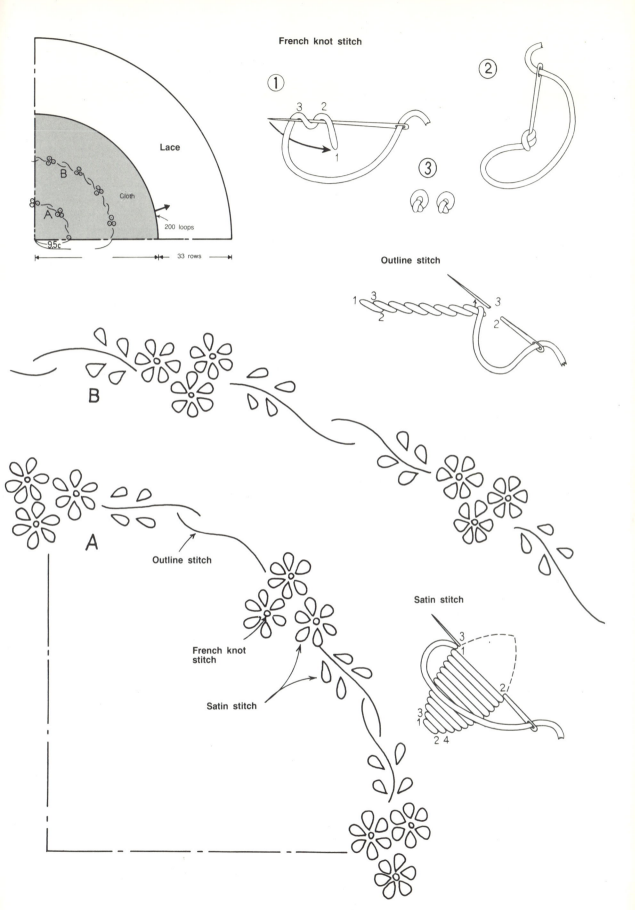

French knot stitch

① ③ ② 1

②

③

Outline stitch

1 3
2
3
2

Lace

Cloth

B

A

9.5c

200 loops

33 rows

B

A

Outline stitch

French knot stitch

Satin stitch

Satin stitch

3 1

2

3 1

2 4

Refreshing Round Tablecloth for the Guest Room

(33) 108 cm in diameter   Instructions on Page 28   (34) 130 cm in diameter   Instructions on Page 32

You'll need:
Crochet cotton DMC No. 40, 350g White (801)
Steel crochet hook:
Crochet hook No. I
Finished size:
130 cm in diameter
Making instructions:
Ch-8, sl st in 1st ch to form a ring. **Row 1:** Ch-5 (1-dc, ch-2) 11 times. **Row 2:** Ch-3, 2-dc-puff, ch-5 (3-dc-puff, ch-5) 11 times. **Rows 3 – 106:** Work net st on Row 3 and 4. From

Row 5, work shell st and net st. From Row 10, work with filet st. Work patterns marked with ◯ on Rows 32 – 35, Rows 40 – 43, and Rows 52 – 55 as shown. From Row 69, work rose patterns. **Rows 107 – 121:** Join thread in. Work in the manner of braid crochet. (Row 1): Ch-5, work (2-dc, ch-2, 2-dc) in ch-2 of Row 106 shell st, ch-2, secure to pattern crochet with sc. Turn, ch-2, work (2-dc, ch-2, 2-dc) in ch-2, continue in same way around the crochet pattern. (Row 2): Join thread in. Ch-1, sc-1, ch-7, sc-1 (ch-8, sc-1) continue in same manner around end, ch-7, sl st.

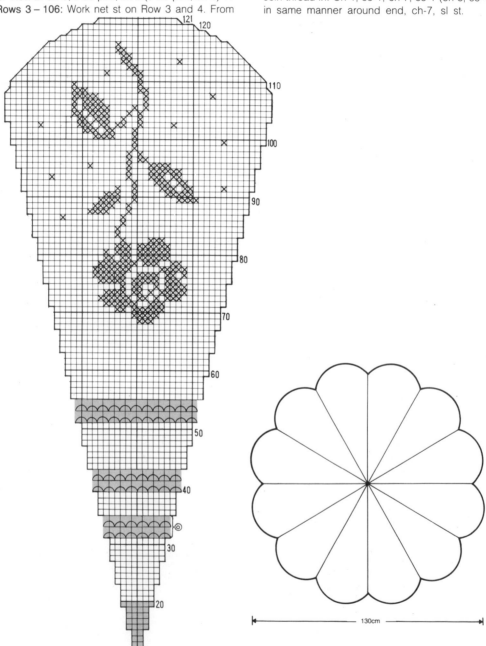

130cm

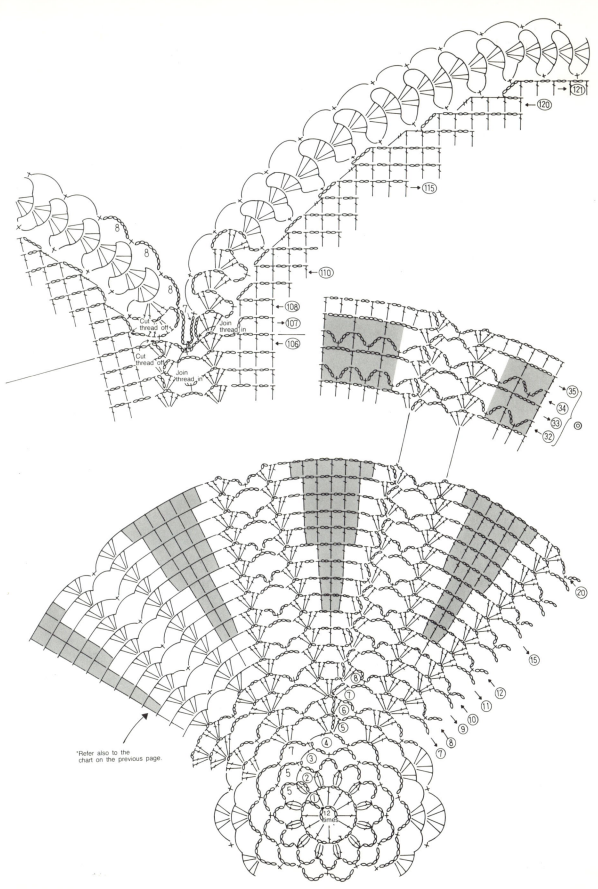

Cut
thread off

Join
thread in

Cut
thread off

Join
thread in

→ 121
← 120
→ 115
← 110
← 108
→ 107
← 106

35
34
33
32

20
15
12
11
10
9
8
7

8
7
6
5
4
3
2
1
12 times

7
5
5

8
7

*Refer also to the
chart on the previous page.

Centerpiece Color Variations
of the Same Motif

(35), (36) Instructions on Page 36

37

Refreshing Argyle Pattern Tablecloth
with Square Pattern

(37) 118 cm × 136 cm   Instructions on Page 76

35. You'll need:

Crochet cotton DMC No. 40, 80g White (801)

Steel crochet hook:

Crochet hook No. I

Finished size:

Hexagon of 4 cm each side

Making instructions:

54 pieces of motif are joined together. Ch-6, sl st in 1st ch to form a ring. **Row 1:** Ch-1 (sc-1, ch-3) 6 times with ch-1, 1-hdc instead of the last ch-3. **Row 2:** Ch-3, 4-dc, ch-9 (1-puff of 5-dc, ch-9) 5 times. **Row 3:** Work 12 loops of net st of ch-5. **Rows 4 – 8:** Work (3-dc, ch-3, 3-dc) in every 5th loop of the net st on Row 3 to form corners of a triangle. Until Row 8, work in accordance with the chart. From the 2nd motif, joining motif while crocheting as shown. Leave 11-ch sts at corner. Ch-6 when working on the 6th motif and return with 1-sc in every 5th loop. Join all 54 pieces of motif and work edging.

36. You'll need:

Crochet cotton DMC No. 40, 30g White (801)

10g rose (121)

Steel crochet hook:

Crochet hook No. I

Finished size:

Hexagon of 22 cm each side

Fringe size:

4 cm

Making instructions:

Work the 8th row of motif (36) with rose colored thread. Join 24 pieces of motif as shown. As for fringe, attach two 12 cm threads at each loop on the last row. Twist a thread with one knot at the end. Cut them to an even length of 4 cm.

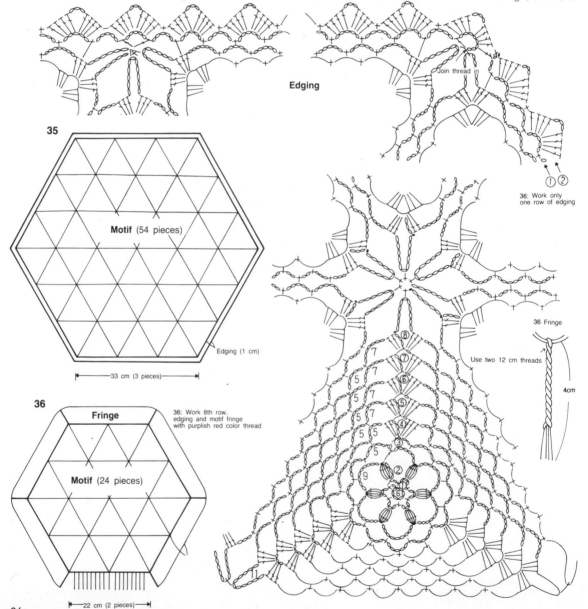

Edging

Join thread in

36: Work only one row of edging

35

Motif (54 pieces)

Edging (1 cm)

|← 33 cm (3 pieces) →|

36

Fringe

Motif (24 pieces)

36: Work 8th row, edging and motif fringe with purplish red color thread

|← 22 cm (2 pieces) →|

36 Fringe

Use two 12 cm threads

4cm

Shown on Page 38

You'll need:
Crochet cotton DMC No. 40, 70g White (801)
Steel crochet hook:
Crochet hook No. I
Finished size:
32 cm × 70 cm

Making instructions:
Ch-187. **Row 1:** Work filet st with 1-dc, ch-2. From 2nd row arrange filet patterns of triangle, square scattered pattern like a patchwork (See chart) without any increase or decrease of sts until 134th row. Work 1 row of edging.

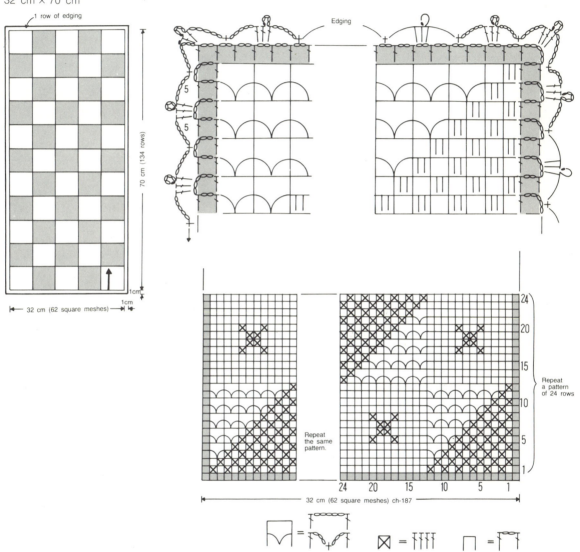

38

Latest Patchwork of Lace

(38) 32 cm × 70 cm   Instructions on Page 37   (39) 33 cm × 70 cm   Instructions on Page 78

38

Shown on Page 42

You'll need:
Centerpiece: Crochet cotton DMC No. 40, 80g, Beige (810)
Pillow: Crochet cotton DMC No. 40, 150g Beige (810) 2 buttons of 1.2 cm in diameter
A brown inner-case, 42 cm by 42 cm stuffed with kapok

Steel crochet hook:
Crochet hook No. I

Finished size:
Centerpiece: 34 cm × 90 cm
Pillow: 42 cm × 42 cm

Making instructions:
Centerpiece: Ch-187. Work until 142th row without any increase or decrease of sts in accordance with charts. Work 2-dc at a time, ch-7 on the first row of edging. **Row 2:** Work net st of ch-7 referring to the chart. **Row 3:** Work fringe at each center of the net st. Be careful not to twist chains.
Pillow: Ch-127. Until 42nd row, work without any decrease of sts referring to the chart. Work 2-dc at a time, ch-7 around. Work net st of ch-7 around. As for the bottom side, ch-127. Work filet st until 42nd row without any increase or decrease of sts. Work 2 rows of edging when working net st on the second row of edging, join to three sides of net st on the top side with sc. Insert the prepared inner-case and stitch opening closed.

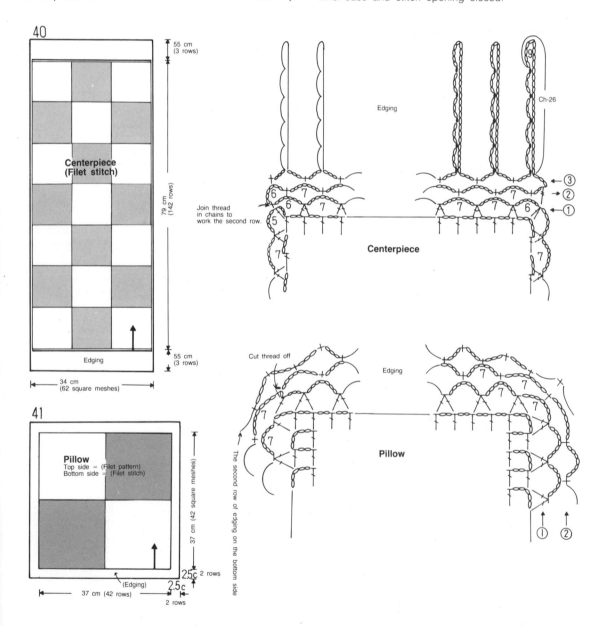

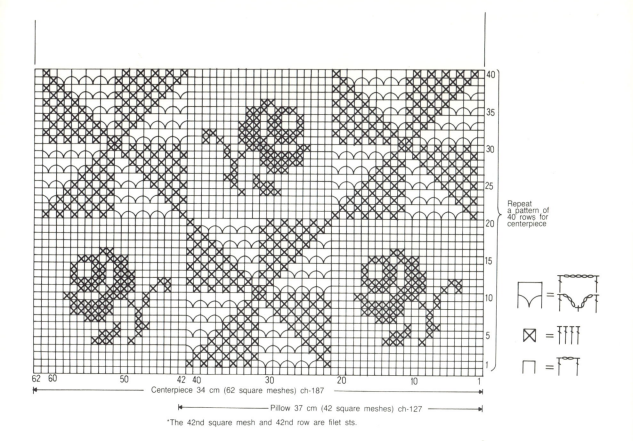

40
35
30

Repeat
a pattern of
40 rows for
centerpiece

25
20
15
10
5
1

62 60   50   42 40   30   20   10   1

Centerpiece 34 cm (62 square meshes) ch-187

Pillow 37 cm (42 square meshes) ch-127

*The 42nd square mesh and 42nd row are filet sts.

How to make a pillow inner-case

In the case of square pillow, stitch a line which goes through a point which is 0.5 cm away from the position dividing a side of the fabric into the ratio of 2 to 1, a curve linking corners. Margin is 1 cm. In the case of a round pillow, cut sides and gores as shown, adding 1 cm margin. In both cases, leave one 20 cm opening for packing kapok. Pack appropriate amount of kapok and stitch opening closed.

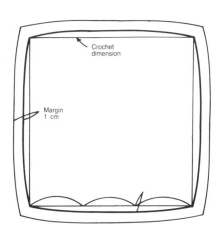

Crochet
dimension

Margin
1 cm

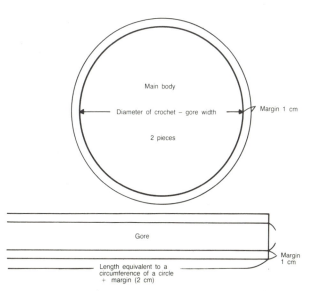

Main body

Diameter of crochet – gore width

Margin 1 cm

2 pieces

Gore

Margin
1 cm

Length equivalent to a
circumference of a circle
+ margin (2 cm)

Latest Patchwork of Lace

(40) 34 cm × 90 cm   (41) 42 cm × 42 cm   Instructions on Page 40

42·43

You'll need:

Centerpiece: Crochet cotton DMC No. 40, 70g White (801)

Pillow:

Crochet cotton DMC No. 40, 130g White (801) A brown satin cloth for an inner-case 90 cm by 90 cm

350g kapok, 2 buttons of 1.2 cm in diameter

Steel crochet hook:

Crochet hook No. I and No. 4

Finished size:

Centerpiece: 36 cm × 78 cm

Pillow: 38 cm × 38 cm, Frill width 3.5 cm

Making instructions:

Centerpiece: Ch-178 using No. I steel crochet hook. Until 135th row, work according to the chart without any increase or decrease of sts. Work 2 rows of edging. Pillow: Ch-152 from the center on the bottom side using No. 4 crochet hook referring to the chart. Work 25 rows of 50 square meshes of filet st. Work 50 rows of the pattern same as the one for centerpiece on the top side as shown in chart on measurement. Work another 24 rows on the bottom side. Finally, work 3 rows. (Row 1) 1-sc, ch-1, alternately. (Row 2) 1-sc (1-sc in ch-1 last row, ch-1) alternately, make 2 buttonholes by ch-3. (Row 3) Same as Row 1. When working 1st row of edging, join the top and bottom sides. From Rows 2 – 6, increase 1 net st at each corner.

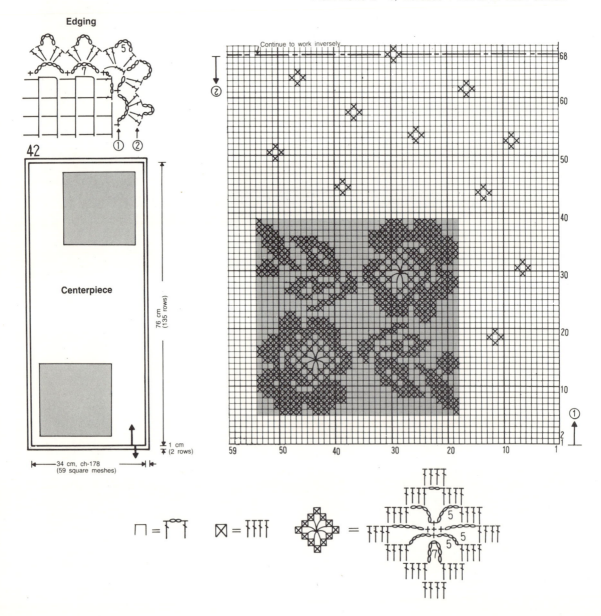

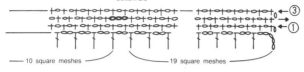

Buttonhole

— 10 square meshes — — 19 square meshes —

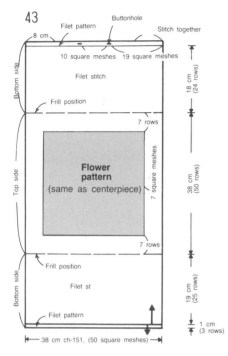

43

8 cm | Filet pattern | Buttonhole | Stitch together

10 square meshes   19 square meshes

Bottom side

Filet stitch

Frill position

7 rows

Flower pattern
(same as centerpiece)

Top side

7 square meshes

7 rows

Frill position

Bottom side

Filet st

Filet pattern

— 38 cm ch-151, (50 square meshes) —

18 cm (24 rows)

38 cm (50 rows)

7 square meshes

19 cm (25 rows)

1 cm (3 rows)

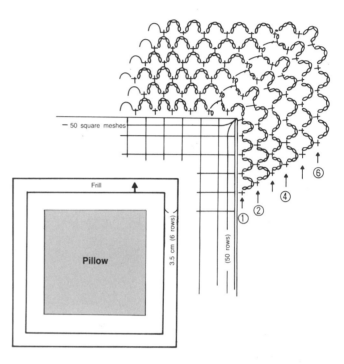

— 50 square meshes

Frill

Pillow

3.5 cm (6 rows)

(50 rows)

① ② ④ ⑥

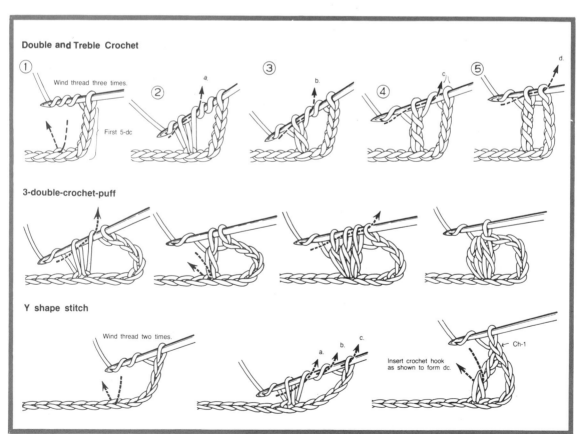

Double and Treble Crochet

① Wind thread three times.

First 5-dc

② a.

③ b.

④ c.

⑤ d.

3-double-crochet-puff

Y shape stitch

Wind thread two times.

a. b. c.

Insert crochet hook as shown to form dc.

Ch-1

Flower Pattern Centerpiece and Pillow

(42) 38 cm × 38 cm (43) 36 cm × 78 cm Instructions on Page 44
(44) 40 cm × 40 cm Instructions on Page 48

You'll need:
Crochet cotton DMC No. 40,100g Pale orange (733) Dark -brown inner-case satin cloth 90 cm by 45 cm, 350g kapok

Steel crochet hook:
Crochet hook No. 4

Finished side:
40 cm × 40 cm

Making instructions:
Ch-148. Start from the center on the bottom side as shown. Work until Row 24. As for the top side, work also filet patterns until Row 49. After working 24 rows on the bottom side, work 3 rows. (Row 1) 1-sc, ch-1, alternately. (Row 2) 1-sc, (1-sc in ch-1 last row, ch-1) alternately, make 2 buttonholes by ch-3)
Cut thread off. Start from the beginning ch, work 3 rows of filet stitch while making buttonholes. Join 8 cm of filet stitch on both sides. Make a case by joining the sides with ch.

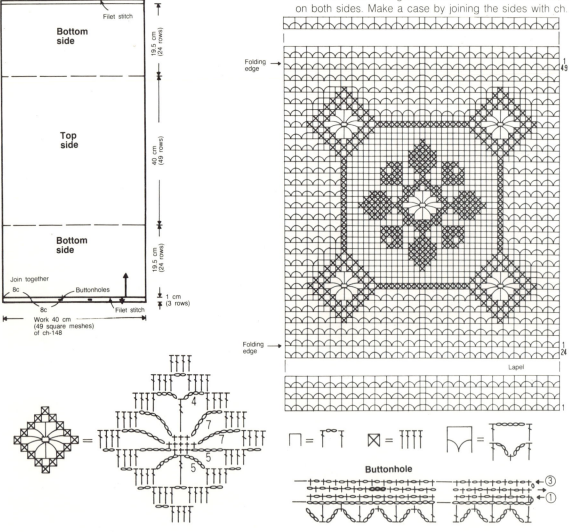

Bottom side

Filet stitch

19.5 cm (24 rows)

Top side

40 cm (49 rows)

Bottom side

19.5 cm (24 rows)

Join together
8c

Buttonholes

8c

Filet stitch

1 cm (3 rows)

Work 40 cm (49 square meshes) of ch-148

Folding edge

Folding edge

Lapel

Buttonhole

Popcorn stitch

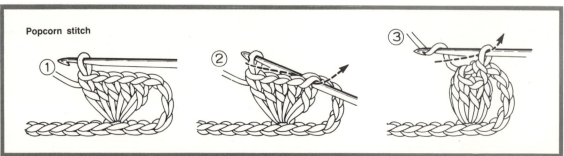

45

Shown on Page 50

You'll need:
Crochet cotton DMC No. 40
A — Beige (810)
B — Pale orange (733) 250g each. Dark brown inner-case satin cloth 55 cm by 110 cm, 400g kapok

Steel crochet hook:
Crochet hook No. 4

Finished size:
51 cm × 51 cm

Making instructions:
Ch-9, sl st in the 1st ch to form a ring. **Row 1:** Ch-3, 23-dc in the ring, sl st in 3rd cts of ch. **Row 2:** Ch-3, 1-dc, ch-5 (2-dc at a time, ch-5) 11 times. **Rows 3 – 7:** Work 5-dc-pop on Row 4. Work dc on Row 7. **Rows 8 – 12:** Start working corner patterns from Row 8. At Row 12, work into a square. Make 9 pieces each for both top and bottom sides, however, from the 2nd piece join motifs at the 12th row. Work one row of net st around. Join top and bottom side together by net st. Insert one inner-case.

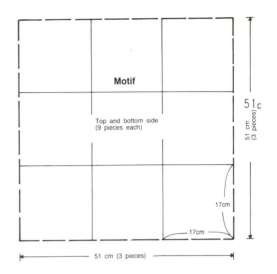

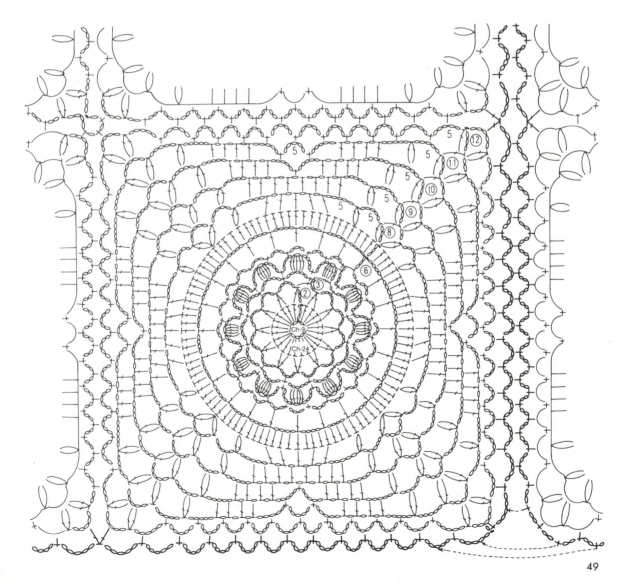

Pillow à la carte

(45) 51 cm × 51 cm Instructions on Page 49   (46) Instructions on Page 79

(47) 43 cm in diameter Instructions on Page 52

You'll need:
Crochet cotton DMC No. 40, 100g Beige (810), Dark brown inner-case satin cloth 90 cm by 45 cm, 400g kapok a 50 cm fine elastic string.

Steel crochet hook:
Crochet hook No. 4

Finished size:
43 cm in diameter

Making instructions:
Ch-8, sl st in 1st ch to form a ring. **Row 1:** Ch-4, 1-tr, ch-3 (2-tr, ch-3) 7 times. **Rows 2 – 20:** Referring to the chart, work 8 pineapple patterns with tr and dc. They may appear to be slackened, but they can be adjusted at the finishing stage. **Rows 21 – 30:** Work 88 patterns of (2-dc, ch-4) without any increase or decrease of sts. **Rows 31 – 34:** Work 88 patterns of (2-dc, ch-3) without any increase or decrease of sts. **Row 35:** Work 88 net sts of ch-7. **Row 36:** Work 88 net sts of ch-10.

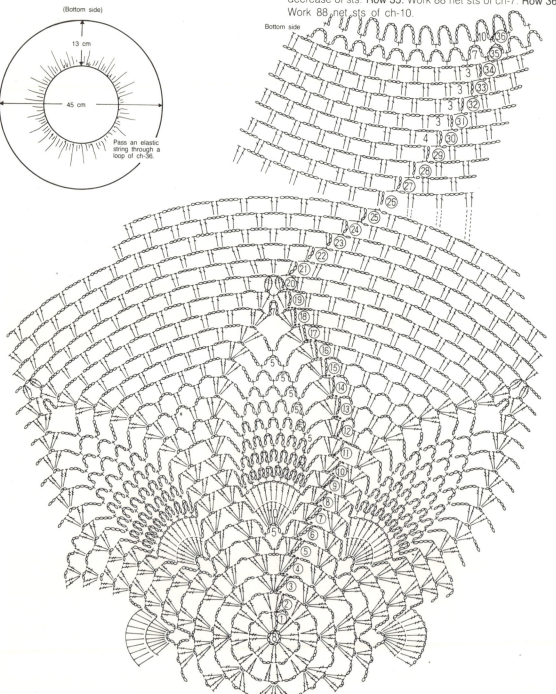

(Bottom side)

13 cm

45 cm

Pass an elastic string through a loop of ch-36.

Bottom side

48~50

You'll need:
Crochet cotton DMC No. 40 White (801) 15g for a tray cloth and about 5g each for a glass mat.

Finished size:
Tray cloth: 20 cm × 25 cm
Glass mat: 20 cm × 12 cm

Making instructions:
Tray cloth: Ch-106. Work filet st in accordance with the chart until Row 45 without any increase, decrease of sts. Work one row of edging around. Glass mat: Ch-64. Work filet st referring to the chart until Row 21 without increase or decrease of sts. Work one row of edging around. 49 and 50 are enlarged charts of the same design.

Edging

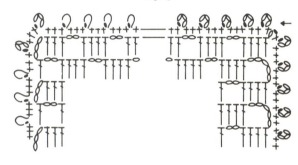

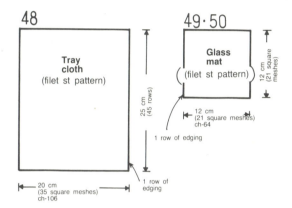

48
Tray cloth (filet st pattern)
25 cm (45 rows)
20 cm (35 square meshes) ch-106
1 row of edging

49·50
Glass mat (filet st pattern)
12 cm (21 square meshes)
12 cm (21 square meshes) ch-64
1 row of edging

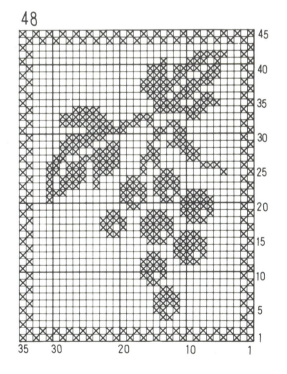

48

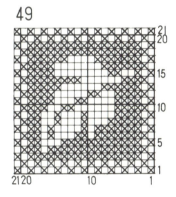

49

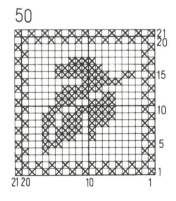

50

$\square$ =
$\boxtimes$ =

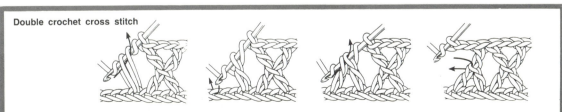

Double crochet cross stitch

Refreshing Tray Cloth and Glass Mats for a Party or a Daily Dining Table

(48) 20 cm × 25 cm   (49), (50) 12 cm × 12 cm   Instructions on Page 53

(51) 5 cm in diameter Instructions on Page 80
(52) 12 cm × 12 cm Instructions on Page 56
(53) 11.5 cm in diameter

51

52

53

55

52. You'll need:
Crochet cotton DMC No. 40, 10g Pink (104)
Steel crochet hook:
Crochet hook No. 4
Finished size:
12 cm × 12 cm
Making instructions:
Make a loop at the end of cotton. **Row 1:** Ch-3, 2-dc, ch-3 (3-dc, ch-3) 3 times. **Rows 2 – 7:** Referring to the chart, increase sts at the corner until Row 4. From Row 5, work net st of ch-5 between patterns. **Row 8:** Work sc and sl st picot around, adjusting shape.

53. You'll need:
Crochet cotton DMC No. 40, 10g White (801)
Steel crochet hook:
Crochet hook No. 4
Finished size:
11.5 cm in diameter
Making instructions:
Make a loop at the end of cotton. **Row 1:** Ch-3, 23-dc in ring, sl st in 3rd sts of beginning ch. **Row 2:** Ch-3, 2-dc, ch-2 (3-dc, ch-2) 7 times. **Rows 3 – 6:** As shown in the chart, increase sts at both sides of dc. On Row 5, ch-1, work filet st. On Row 6, ch-3, 6-dc, ch-3, 1-sc (7-dc, ch-3, 1-sc) around. **Row 7:** Repeat chain picot and dc on dc with ch-7 between patterns.

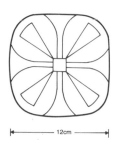

|← 12cm →|

|← 11.5cm →|

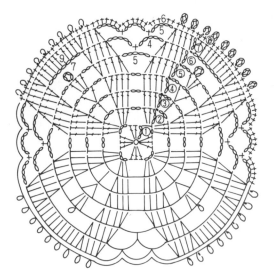

You'll need:
Crochet cotton DMC No. 40, 180g White (801)
Steel crochet hook:
Crochet hook No. I.
Finished size:
50 cm × 120 cm
Making instructions:
Ch-124. In accordance with the chart, work pattern st of fringe. Continue to work filet st. Work 207 rows and start edging.
Instructions for edging:
Join a thread to (1). Ch-6, 1 quintuple treble crochet at a time. Then, ch-6, work in the st of 3-dc at a time. Work 1 quintuple treble crochet, ch-5, 2 quintuple treble crochet at a time to make a pattern. Ch-3, then move to the second pattern. Wind (a) and (b) shown in the chart both at a same time (10 windings) then return 5 windings of (b). Together with quintuple treble crochet of (c), (d), (e), work 4 stitches together. Then, return 5 windings of (a). Work quintuple treble crochet of (f) in a position with previous 4 stitches. Work 2 stitches (d) and (f) together. Then, ch-5, work 2 quintuple treble crochet (g) and (h) together. Join thread to (2). Ch-8, work a row of shell st. Put a bar through the holes of edging.

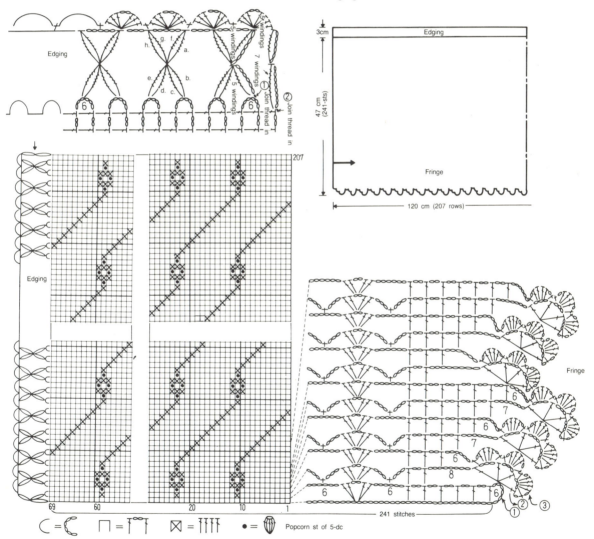

Popcorn st of 5-dc

Room dividers (54) 50 cm × 120 cm Instructions on Page 57
(55) 45 cm × 90 cm Instructions on Page 81

You'll need:
Crochet cotton DMC No. 40 10g White (801)
Steel crochet hook:
Crochet hook No. I
Finished size:
40 cm in diameter
Making instructions:
Ch-5, sl st in 1-st ch to form a ring. **Row 1:** Ch-5 (1-dc, ch-2) 9 times. **Rows 2 – 5:** As shown in the chart, on Row 2, ch-3, 1-dc, ch-3 (2-dc, ch-3) 9 times. On **Row 5:** Repeat (7-dc, ch-3, 7-dc) 10 times in loop. **Rows 6 – 10:** Work 5 rows of net st of ch-5 without increase or decrease sts. (40 loops per round) **Rows 11 – 13:** On Row 11, ch-3, 2-dc ch-7 (3-dc, ch-7) 39 times in previous loops. On Row 13, (1-dc, ch-1) 9 times in a loop of ch-7 on the previous row. Work shell st between patterns around. Cut thread off. **Rows 14 – 25:** Join a new thread as the starting position will be different. Work pineapple patterns referring to the chart. **Rows 26 – 33:** Work 8 rows of net st of ch-5 (120 loops per round). **Rows 34, 35:** Work 3-dc in each loop on previous row. Work ch-10 and ch-1 between patterns alternatively. Work (7-dc, ch-3, 7-dc) in ch-10.

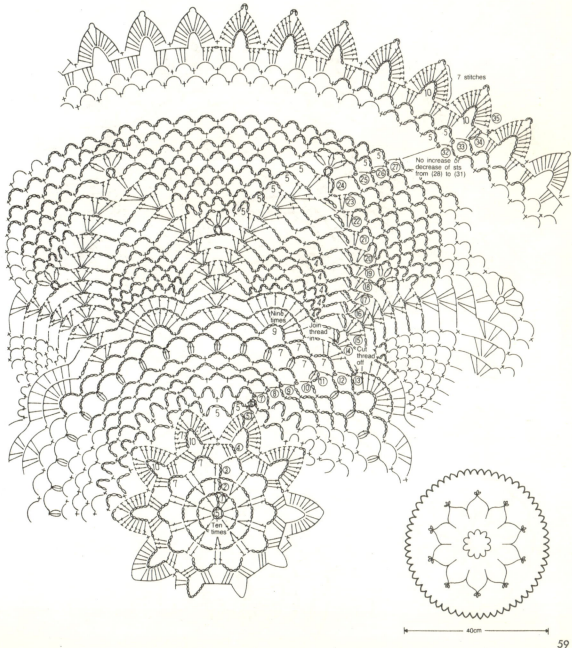

2

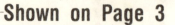

You'll need:
Crochet cotton DMC No. 40, 30g White (801)
Steel crochet hook:
Crochet hook No. I
Finished size:
36 cm in diameter
Making instructions:
Ch-10, sl st in 1st ch to form a ring. **Row 1:** Ch-3, 23-dc in ring, sl st in 3rd s of ch. **Rows 2 – 5:** Work 24 square meshes of dc and ch. The number of chs increases every row. **Rows 6 – 8:** As shown in the chart, increase stitches at the position of dc. **Row 8:** Work shape st of 1-dc, ch-2, 1-dc. 3 chains between V shape sts at every row. **Rows**

9 – 12: Work shell st (2-dc, ch-2, 2-dc) in every other V shape st increasing sts of ch until Row 12. **Rows 13 – 18:** Work ch-3 in shell st on Row 13 instead of ch-2. From Row 14, divide shell sts into two. Work 8-tr around to make 12 patterns as the base of pineapple pattern on Row 18. **Rows 19 – 24:** In accordance with the chart work a part of V shape st until Row. 23. **Row 24:** Work (1-tr, ch-4, 1-tr) into V shape patterns. **Row 25:** Work 8-dc in (1-tr, ch-4, 1-tr) on the Row 24. **Rows 26 – 30:** Expand dc radially increasing sts of ch. **Rows 31, 32:** Work 2-dc in dc on Row 30. **Row 32:** Repeat (1-dc, ch-3, 1-dc, ch-2). **Row 33:** Repeat (3-dc, 4-ch-p (sl st at the end p), 2-dc, ch-1) to make 108 patterns around.

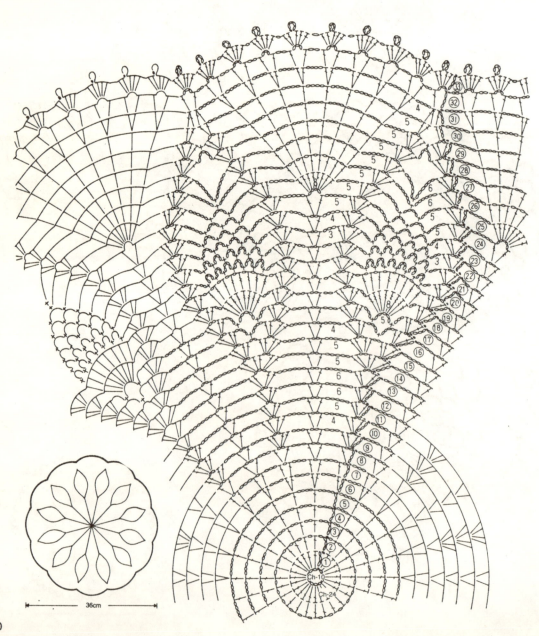

36cm

3

You'll need:

Crochet cotton DMC No. 40, 30g White (801)

Steel crochet hook:

Crochet hook No. I

Finished size: 33 cm in diameter

Making instructions:

Ch-6, sl st in 1st ch to form a ring. **Row 1:** Ch-3, 23-dc, sl st in 3rd st of beginning ch. **Row 2:** Ch-4 (1-dc, ch-1) 23 times. **Row 3:** Ch-8 (1-dc, ch-5) 23 times. **Rows 4 – 9:** Work 3 rows of net st of ch-5, and 3 rows of net st of ch-6. **Row 10:** Work (3-dc, ch-2, 3-dc) in each loop on the previous row to make 24 patterns around. **Row 11:** As shown in the chart, work 1 shell st, (2-dc, ch-2, 2-dc), ch-5, 1-sc, ch-7, 1-sc, ch-5 8

times. **Rows 12 – 16:** Make the base of pineapple pattern working 10-dc in loops at ch-7 on the previous row. Work 1.5 patterns of shell, and divide it into 2 patterns on Row 13. **Rows 17 – 25:** Work pineapple pattern decreasing 1 loop of net st of ch-4 at every row. As shown in the chart, increase 1 loop of ch-5 net st at every row between shells. On Row 25, work pattern of 1 puff (3-dc at a time), ch-3 1 puff twice in 8 places. **Rows 26 – 34:** Referring to the chart, work 1 puff, ch-3, 1 puff twice of Row 25 on Rows 28 and 31. For the rest, work net st (1-sc, ch-6 or 7). **Row 35:** Work 1-dc, ch-3, 1-dc in each loop on the previous row and ch-6 (80 patterns around). **Row 36:** Work 3-dc-puff with 5-ch-p (sl st at the end p).

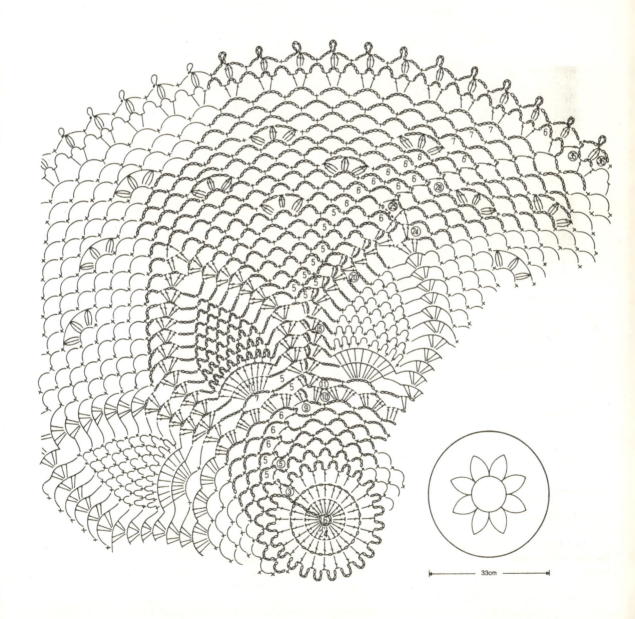

33cm

You'll need:
Crochet cotton DMC No. 40, 20g White (801)
Steel crochet hook:
Crochet hook No. I
Finished size: 28 cm in diameter
Making instructions:
Make a loop at the end of cotton. **Row 1:** Ch-9, (1-tr, ch-5) 7 times. (End with ch-2, 1-dc). **Row 2:** Work net st (1-sc, ch-5). **Rows 3 – 10:** On Row 3, work shell st of (2-dc, ch-2, 2-dc) in loops on the previous row with ch-5 between shells.

Continue shell st radiately until Row 11. From Row 6, work 2 more shell sts between previous shell sts. **Rows 11 – 23:** From Row 12, divide shell sts stitched radiately into V shape. From Row 18, work 2 more shell sts between them. **Rows 11 and 12:** As shown in the chart, work chevron patterns between sts worked radiately. **Rows 13 – 22:** Work pineapple pattern of ch-4. **Rows 24 – 26:** In accordance with the chart, work small fan shape patterns on top of the pineapple patterns and large fan shape pattern between patterns. Finish working with ch-p on the last row.

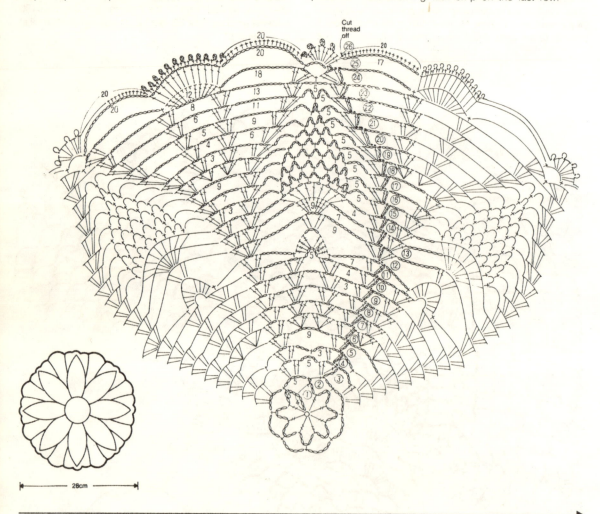

You'll need:
Crochet cotton DMC No. 40, 20g White (801)
Steel crochet hook:
Crochet hook No. I
Finished size: 32 cm in diameter
Making instructions:
Motif — Ch-8, sl st in 1st ch to form a ring. **Row 1:** Ch-1, 12-sc in ring, sl st in 1st ch. **Row 2:** Work 6 loops of net st (1-sc, ch-5) in every other st. **Row 3:** Work 1-sc, 3-dc, ch-2, 3-dc, 1-sc in loops on the previous row. From the second piece on, join work in accordance with the chart on

measurement. Join 19 pieces.
Outside — Row 1: Work ch-10 in each loop around. (30 loops) **Rows 2 – 13:** Work 4-tr together, ch-10 on Row 2 increasing sts at 6 places as shown. Work 8-dc in every fourth loop on the previous row to form the base for pineapple pattern. Work shell st around to separate 8 patterns. Join with ch sts until Row 7. From Row 8, work net st (1-sc, ch-5). **Rows 14 – 17:** Work 96 loops of net st (1-sc, ch-5) on 1 row and make two rows of net st (1-sc, ch-6). **Row 17:** Work ch-3, ch-3-p (sl st at the end p), ch-3 around.

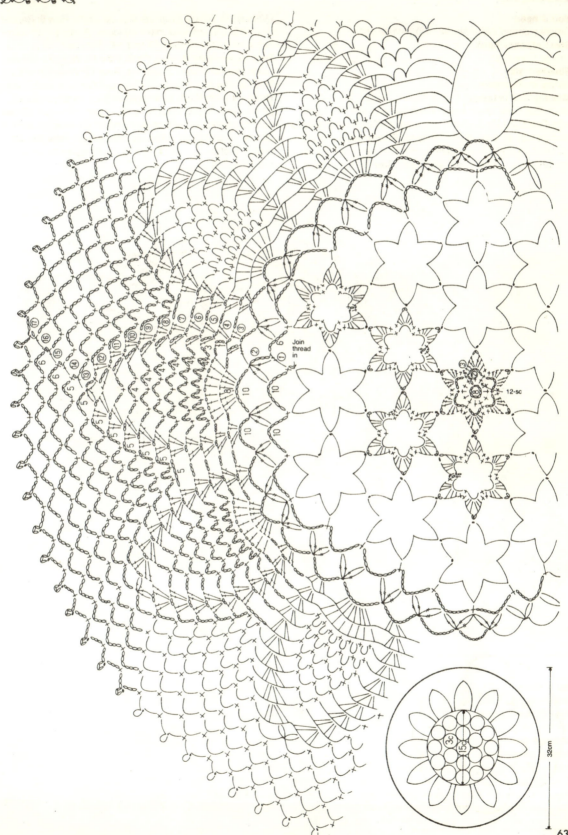

Join thread in

12-sc

3c

15c

32cm

You'll need:
Crochet cotton DMC No. 40, 30g White (801)
Steel crochet hook:
Crochet hook No. I
Finished size:
33 cm in diameter
Making instructions:
Ch-6, sl st in 1st ch to form a ring. **Row 1:** Ch-6, 1-tr tr (triple treble crochet), ch-7, (2-tr tr at a time, ch-7) 11 times. **Row 2:** Work net st (1-sc, ch-9) 12 times. **Row 3:** Work 2-dc, tr together (double treble crochet), ch-7 twice in each loop on the previous row to make 24 loops. **Row 4:** Work net st (1-sc, ch-7). **Row 5:** Work net st (1-sc, ch-8). **Row 6:** Repeat 2-dtr together, ch-7 to make 48 loops. **Rows 7 – 15:** Work net st as shown. **Rows 13 and 14:** Work with dtr and ch. **Row 15:** Work net st (1-sc, ch-9). **Row 16:** Work 9-tr in every fourth loop to make 12 patterns. **Row 17:** Work 1-tr, ch-1 9 times on top of the base of pineapple on the previous row. **Rows 18 – 24:** Work pineapple of 3-dc together between pineapples started from Row 16. Work alternately. **Rows 25 – 27:** Work 1-dc and ch-4 as shown. On Row 25, work in ch. On Rows 26, 27: Work in loops of ch. **Row 28:** Work 3-sc, 1-sl st picot of ch-3, 3-sc in each square mesh on the previous row.

You'll need:
Crochet cotton DMC No. 40, 40g White (801)
Steel crochet hook:
Crochet hook No. I
Finished size:
40 cm in diameter

Making instructions:
Work around on the first 40 rows. From Row 41, work turning each round for each pattern. Ch-8, sl st in 1st ch to form a ring. **Row 1:** Ch-3, 23-dc in ring, sl st in 3rd st of beginning ch. **Row 2:** Ch-4, (1-sc, 1-ch) 23 times. **Rows 3 – 8:** Work net st increasing sts of ch. **Row 9:** Work shell st and net st alternately. **Row 10:** Ch-5 in every other shell on the previous row to make the base for pineapple patterns. **Rows 11 – 26:** Work 15-tr in shell st of ch-5 to make 6 patterns. From Row 22, start working second pineapple patterns between first ones. **Rows 27 – 40:** Work 3rd pineapple patterns from Row 35. **Rows 41 – 51:** Work a pineapple pattern one at a time.

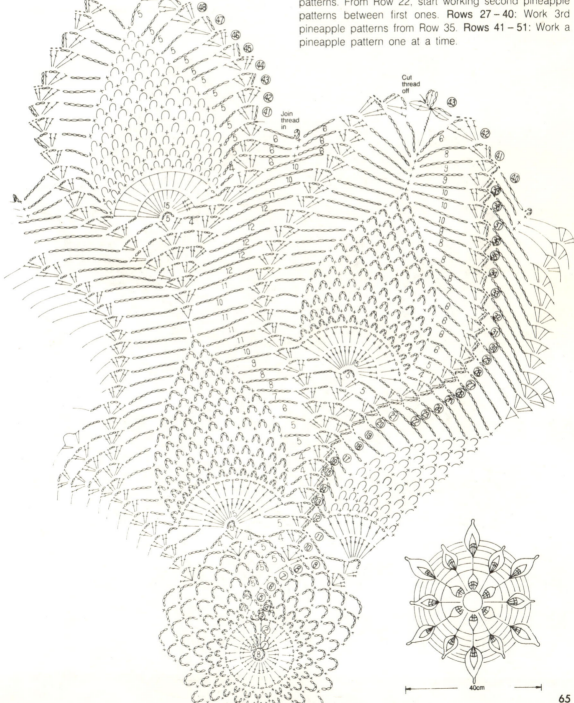

40cm

You'll need:
Crochet cotton DMC No. 40, 30g White (801)
Steel crochet hook:
Crochet hook No. I
Finished size:
38 cm in diameter
Making instructions:
Ch-12, sl st in 1st ch to form a ring. **Row 1:** Ch-3, 23-dc in ring, sl st in 3rd st of beginning ch. **Row 2 – 4:** As shown in chart, work dc and ch to make 24 square meshes on each row increasing sts to ch. **Row 5:** Work 12 V shape pattern sts of 1-dc, ch-2, 1-dc in every other dc on the previous row with ch and dc between them. **Rows 6– 26:** Work 3-dc-puff, ch-2, 3-dc-puff on top of V shape pattern sts until Row 15, increasing sts of ch. On Row 9, work V shape pattern sts of 1-dc, ch-1, 1-dc and make the 1st base of pineapple pattern (7-tr) on Row 13 in accordance with the chart. Second pineapple patterns start from Row 19. Work around until Row 26. **Rows 27 – 31:** From Row 27, join thread to each pineapple pattern and work turning each row until Row 31 to make 12 pineapple patterns. Work p around and adjust the shape.

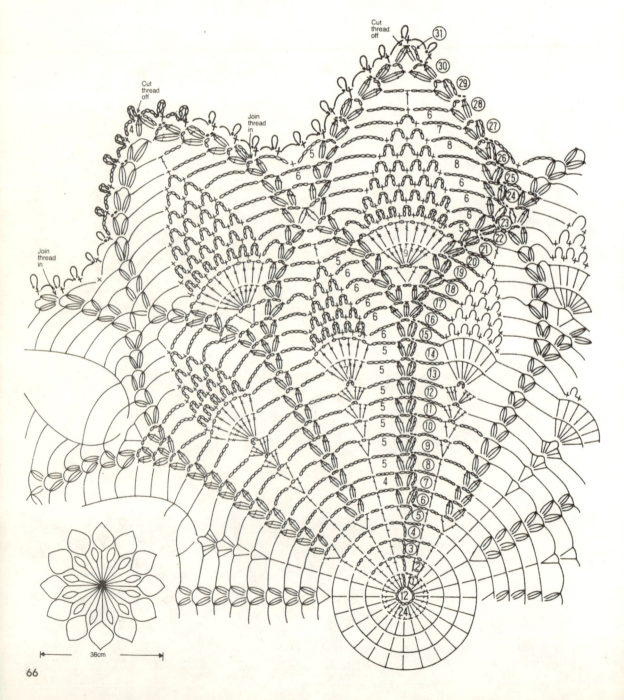

9

You'll need:
Crochet cotton DMC No. 40, 10g White (801)
Steel crochet hook:
Crochet hook No. I
Finished size:
24 cm in diameter
Making instructions:
Motif — Ch-10, sl st in 1st ch to form a ring. **Row 1:**
Alternately repeat 4-dc-puff, ch-15 and 4-dc-puff, ch-7 3
times to make triangle. **Row 2:** Work ch-5, 3-dc-puff, ch-5 5
times in net st (1-sc, ch-15). **Row 3:** Work net st (1-sc, ch-5)
to make 18 loops. In making 6 pieces of this motif, join 5

loops on the side of a triangle with sc from the second motif.
In the same manner, 6 pieces are joined to form hexagon.
Central opening is filled with pieces.
Piece — Ch-10, sl st in 1st ch to form a ring. Repeat
4-dc-puff, ch-3 and 1-sc in a loop at the top of motif, ch-3 6
times.
Outside motif — **Row 1:** Work net st (1-sc, ch-15) in every
other loop of net st (1-sc, ch-5) of the motif outside to make
24 loops. **Row 2:** As shown in the chart, work 3-dc-puff 3
times in each loop of net st (1-sc, ch-15) on the previous
row with ch-5 between puffs. **Rows 3 – 10:** Work 72 loops of
net st on each row, increasing sts of ch.

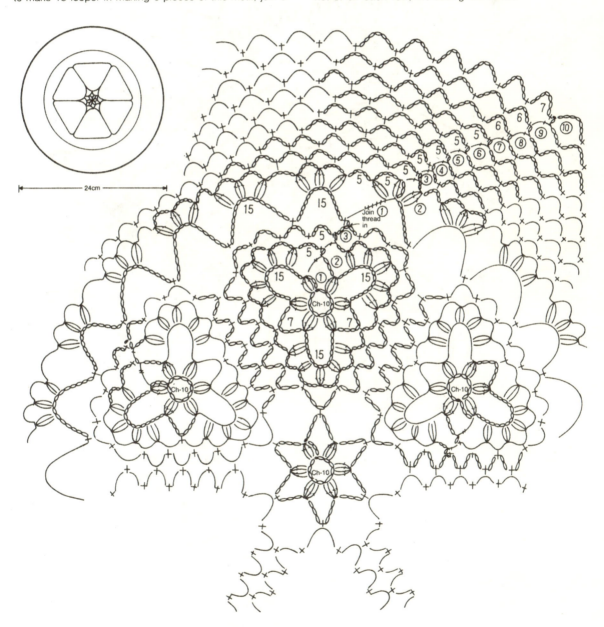

You'll need:

Crochet cotton DMC No. 40, 10g White (801)

Steel crochet hook:

Crochet hook No. I

Finished size: 22 cm in diameter

Making instructions:

Ch-6, sl st in 1st ch to form a ring. **Row 1:** Ch-4, (1-dc, ch-1)

11 times. **Rows 2 – 8:** Make filet crochet repeating the same method as in Rows 2 and 3, increasing sts in 6 places. **Rows 9 – 16:** In accordance with the chart, work pattern st on a line extending from increased sts at corners and a center of a side. **Row 17:** Repeat 1-dc, ch-5 120 times and adjust the shape of crochet. **Row 18:** Work 2-dc, a loop of ch-5 on the previous row and ch-10.

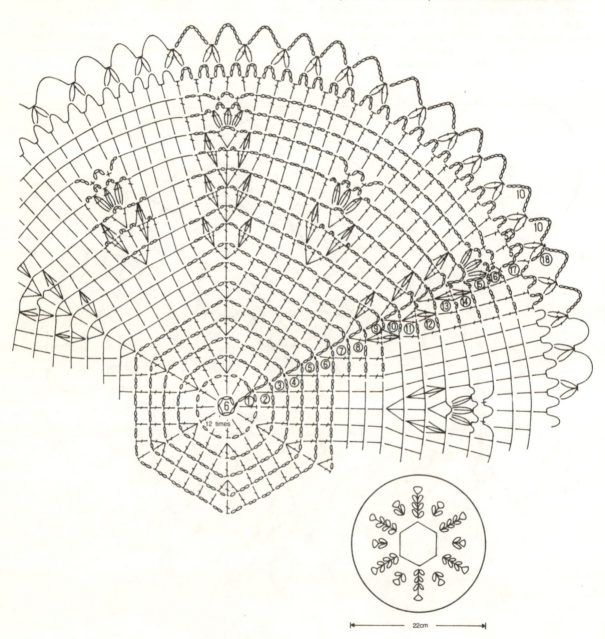

12 times

22cm

You'll need:
Crochet cotton DMC No. 40, 10g Beige (733)
Steel crochet hook:
Crochet hook No. I
Finished size:
26 cm in diameter
Making instructions:
Motif — Ch-8, sl st in 1-st ch to form a ring. **Row 1**: Ch-7, (1-dc, ch-4) 5 times. **Row 2**: Work 1-sc, ch-1, 3-dc, ch-1, 3-dc, ch-1, 1-sc to make 6 petals. **Row 3**: 1-ch, 1-sc, ch-13. Work sc in the central ch of petals. Work 19 pieces of

hexagon motif. From the second piece, refer to the chart on measurement. On Row 3, work (ch-6, 1-sc) to join with a side (ch-13) of the 1st motif. Then, work ch-6. In the same way, join all 19 pieces.

Edging — **Row 1**: Work 1 quintuple treble crochet, ch-3, 1 quintuple treble crochet between the connecting portion of two pieces of motif. Work ch-9 on both sides, and ch-13 in corners only. **Rows 2 – 3**: Work net st of ch-9 to form 48 loops. **Row 4**: Work 4-dc-puff in net st on the previous row, ch-10, then, 2-dc-puff, ch-3. Work sl st at the foot of puff and ch-7 to make 48 patterns around.

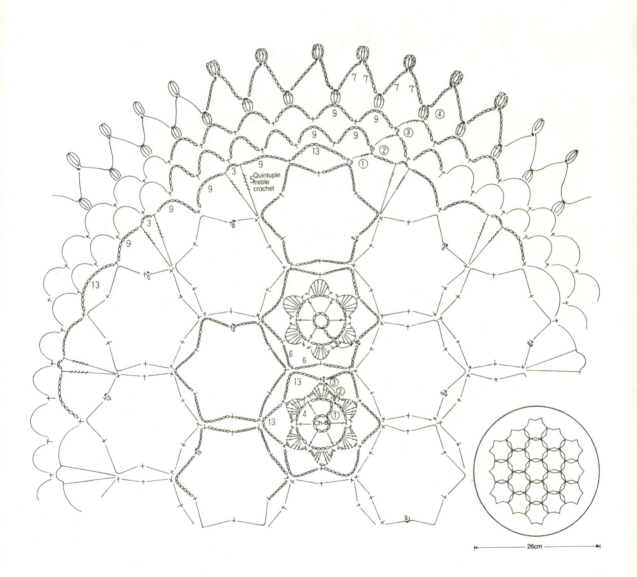

26cm

20 ─────────────────────────────────

You'll need:
Crochet cotton DMC No. 40, 10g, Beige (733)
Steel crochet hook:
Crochet hook No. I
Finished size: 25 cm in diameter
Making instructions:
Ch-8, sl st in 1st ch to form a ring. **Row 1:** Ch-4, (1-dc, ch-1) 11 times. **Row 2:** Ch-3, work sl st in ch-1 on the previous row. **Row 3:** Work net st (1-sc, ch-5), and work sc in sl st sts on the previous row. **Row 4:** Work one 4-tr-puff in each loop of net st on the previous row with ch-7 between. **Row 5:** Work net st (1-sc, ch-9) to form 12 loops. **Rows 6 – 12:** In accordance with the chart, work petal patterns. **Rows 13 – 20:** Work net st (1-sc, ch-7). On only Row 16, work 3-tr-puff, ch-5, 3-tr-puff in every 5th loop in 12 places. **Row 21:** Work ch-2, 1-sc, ch-5, 1-sc in net st (1-sc, ch-7) on the previous row. **Row 22:** Work shell st of 3-dc, ch-3, 3-dc in ch-2 to make 60 patterns.

25cm

19 **Shown on Page 22**

You'll need:
Crochet cotton DMC No. 40, 20g White (801)
Steel crochet hook:
Crochet hook No. I
Finished size:
33 cm in diameter
Making instructions:
Continue to work from Row 20 of 10g doily (20). **Row 21:**

Work net st (1-sc, ch-7) to make 60 loops. **Row 22:** Work patterns between the previously worked pattern following the same procedure as in Row 16 shown in the chart. **Rows 23 – 26:** Work net st (1-sc, ch-7) to make 72 loops. **Row 27:** Work ch-1, 3-tr-puff, ch-5, 3-tr-puff ch-5, 3-tr-puff, ch-1 in every other loop of net st on the previous row to make 36 patterns. **Row 28:** Work 1-sc in ch-1 on the previous row and 3-sc in ch-5, 1-ch-4, p, 2-sc around.

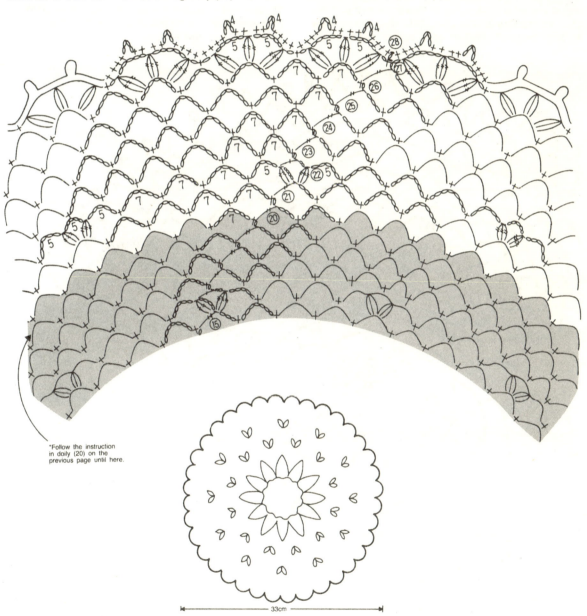

*Follow the instruction in doily (20) on the previous page until here.

├─────── 33cm ───────┤

You'll need:
Crochet cotton DMC No. 40, 10g, clean (520)
Steel crochet hook:
Crochet hook No. I
Finished size:
24 cm in diameter
Making instructions:
Ch-8, sl st in 1st ch to form a ring. **Row 1:** Ch-3, 23-dc in ring, sl st in 3rd st of beginning ch. **Row 2:** Work ch-4, (1-dc, ch-1) around. **Row 3:** Work ch-5, (1-dc, ch-2) around. **Row 4:** Work 3-dc-puff, ch-3 in each square mesh on the previous row 24 times. **Row 5:** Make net st (1-sc, ch-5) to form 24 loops. **Row 6:** Work 4-dc, ch-3, 4-dc in every other loop of net st on the previous row to make 12 patterns. **Row 7:** Work ch-13 and 1-sc in pine tree st on the previous row around. **Rows 8 – 19:** In accordance with the chart, make 12 patterns with dc from Row 18. Dc on Row 8 is worked in sts of ch on the previous row; however, dc in a diaper pattern starting from Row 14 is worked in loops of ch. **Row 20:** Work net st of ch-5 to make 96 loops. **Row 21:** Work ch-3, 4-ch-p (sl st at the end p), ch-2 and stitch it to net st on the previous row with sc.

23·24·25

23. You'll need:
Crochet cotton DMC No. 40, 10g White, (801)
A cotton handkerchief white 38 cm by 38 cm.
Steel crochet hook:
Crochet hook No. I
Finished size: 2.7 cm in width
Making instructions:
Row 1: Work net st of 1-sc, ch-5 56 times on each side. Work net st (1-sc, ch-3) at each corner. Rows 2 – 4: One pattern has 7 loops of net st. Decrease a loop of net st at each row, while increasing sts of 3-dc-puff. Row 5: As shown in the chart, work 3-dc-puff and net st with 3-ch-p (sl st at the end p) around.

24. You'll need:
Crochet cotton DMC No. 40, 10g, White (801)
A white cotton handkerchief, 38 cm by 38 cm.
Steel crochet hook:
Crochet hook No. I
Finished size:
2.7 cm in width
Making instructions:
Row 1: Work sc-1, ch-7 37 times on each side. Work sc-1,

ch-7 once at each corner. End with a loop of ch-4 and 1-dc.
Rows 2 – 5: One pattern has 3 loops of net st. Referring to the chart, make the base for pineapple pattern working 1-dc, ch-1 5 times. Work ch-5 to make the base for filet stitch (consist of dc and ch) alternately. Work ch-3 for pineapple pattern. Decrease the number of loops. Increase the number of sts in filet stitch. Row 6: Work around ch-3, 1-dc in each dc.

25. You'll need:
Crochet cotton DMC No. 40, 10g, White (801)
A white cotton handkerchief, 38 cm by 38 cm.
Steel crochet hook:
Crochet hook No. I
Finished size:
2 cm in width
Making instructions:
Row 1: Work 1-dc, ch-7 38 times on each side. Work 1-sc, ch-7 once at a corner. End with a loop of ch-4 and 1-dc. Row 2: Repeat a pattern of ch-5, 1-sc, ch-3, 1-sc around, however, work 1-sc, ch-5 once at each corner. Row 3: Same as Row 1. Row 4: Same as Row 2. Row 5: Work net st (1-sc, ch-7) around.

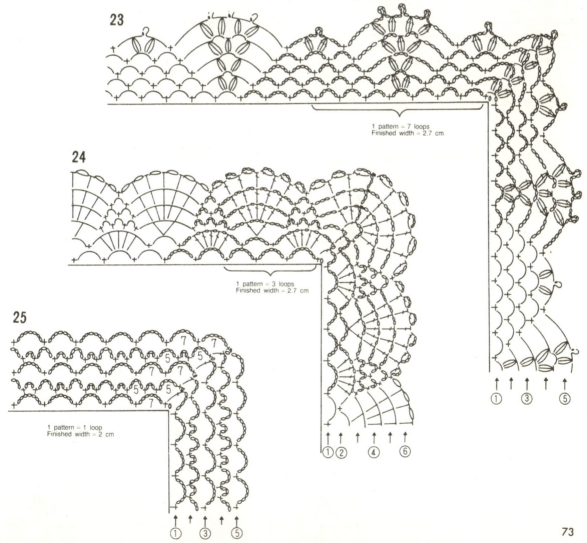

1 pattern = 7 loops
Finished width = 2.7 cm

1 pattern = 3 loops
Finished width = 2.7 cm

1 pattern = 1 loop
Finished width = 2 cm

28. You'll need:

Crochet cotton DMC No. 40, 10g, Pink (104)
A cotton handkerchief, check pattern, 36 cm by 36 cm.

Steel crochet hook:

Crochet hook No. I

Finished size: 1.5 cm in width

Making instructions:

Row 1: Work 1-sc, ch-5 51 times (multiple of 3) on each side, and 1-sc, ch-5 once at each corner. End with a loop of ch-3 and 1-hdc. **Row 2:** Work ch-5, stitch it to a loop on the previous row. Work 2-dc, ch-3 stitched with 1-sc, ch-3, 2-dc in the next loop on the previous row. Work net st (1-sc, ch-5) and the pattern st of 2-dc, ch-3 stitched with 1-sc, ch-3, 2-dc around. Make 1 loop of net st at a corner. **Row 3:** Work 3-ch-p (sl st at the end p) in every 3rd loop with net st (1-sc, ch-5).

29. You'll need:

Crochet cotton DMC No. 40, 10g, Light blue (383)
Cotton handkerchief, check pattern, 36 cm by 36 cm.

Steel crochet hook:

Crochet hook No. I

Finished size:

1.5 cm in width

Making instructions:

Row 1: Work 1-sc, ch-5 51 times (multiple of 3) on each side, while working 1-sc, ch-5 once at each corner. End with a loop of ch-2 and 1-dc. **Row 2:** Work ch-3, 2-dc, ch-3 in each loop at corner. As 1 pattern has 3 loops, repeat 2 loops of net st (1-sc, ch-5), 2-dc, ch-3, 1-sc around. **Row 3:** Repeat 2 loops of net st (1-sc, ch-5), ch-3, 2-dc, 1-sc

Work sc-1 at each corner and make the same as Row 2 on around. Make the same as Row 2 at each corner. **Row 4:** each side.

30. You'll need:

Crochet cotton DMC No. 40, 10g Blue (366)
A cotton handkerchief, check pattern 36 cm by 36 cm.

Steel crochet hook:

Crochet hook No. I

Finished size:

1.5 cm in width

Making instructions:

Row 1: Work 1-sc, ch-5 47 times on each side, while working 1-sc, ch-5 once at each corner. End with a loop of ch-2 and 1-dc. **Row 2:** Work 3-dc-puff, ch-5 once in each loop on the previous row, and three times in loops at the corner. **Row 3:** Work net st (1-sc, ch-5) around.

31. You'll need:

Crochet cotton DMC No. 40, 10g Gradation (M4)
A cotton handkerchief, check pattern, 36 cm by 36 cm.

Steel crochet hook:

Crochet hook No. I

Finished size:

1 cm in width

Making instructions:

Row 1: Work 1-sc, ch-5 50 times on each side, while working once at each corner. End with a loop of ch-3 and 1-hdc. **Row 2:** Work 1-sc, ch-5 around. Make it twice in loops at corners. **Row 3:** Work 2-dc, 3-ch-p (sl st at the end p), 1-dc in sc on the previous row and join with 1-sc to loops.

28

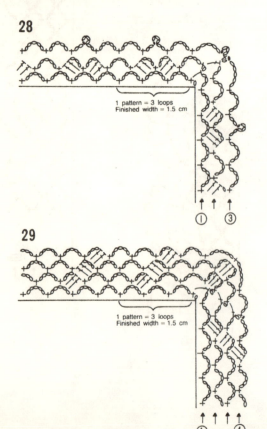

1 pattern = 3 loops
Finished width = 1.5 cm

29

1 pattern = 3 loops
Finished width = 1.5 cm

30

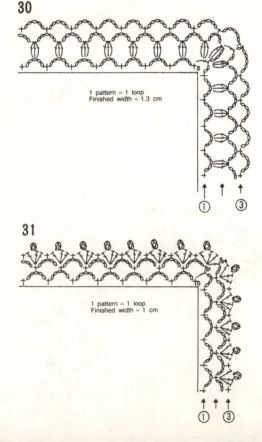

1 pattern = 1 loop
Finished width = 1.3 cm

31

1 pattern = 1 loop
Finished width = 1 cm

26·27·32

26. You'll need:
Crochet cotton DMC No. 40, 10g White (801)
A cotton handkerchief white 38 cm by 38 cm.
Steel crochet hook:
Crochet hook No. I
Finished size:
2.5 cm in width
Making instructions:
Row 1: Work 1-sc, ch-5 54 times on each side. End with a loop of ch-2 and 1-dc. **Rows 2 – 5:** 5 loops make 1 pattern. As shown, make 2-dc, ch-2, 1-dc, ch-2, 2-dc as the base of flower. Work 2-dc, ch-2, 1-dc, ch-2, 2-dc in sts of ch of loops on the previous row. Decrease loops of net st while increasing sts in flower patterns.

27. You'll need:
Crochet cotton DMC No. 40, 10g White (801)
A cotton handkerchief, white, 38 cm by 38 cm.
Steel crochet hook:
Crochet hook No. I
Finished size:
1.5 cm in width
Making instructions:
Row 1: Work 1-sc, ch-7 40 times on each side, while working it once at each corner. **Row 2:** Work ch-6, 1-sc, ch-3, and repeat (1-dc, ch-3, 1-sc, ch-3), while making 1-sc, ch-7 once at each corner. **Row 3:** Work ch-3, 2-dc-puff twice in each pattern on the previous row. **Row 4:** Work 1-sc between puffs, and make net st (1-sc, ch-7).

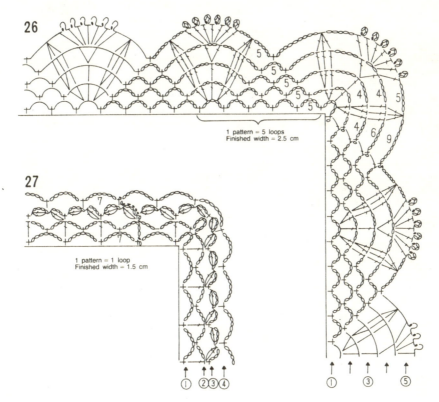

1 pattern = 5 loops
Finished width = 2.5 cm

1 pattern = 1 loop
Finished width = 1.5 cm

32. You'll need:
Crochet cotton DMC No. 40, 10g, Cream (520)
A cotton handkerchief, cream, 32 cm by 32 cm.
Steel crochet hook:
Crochet hook No. I
Finished size:
1.2 cm in width
Making instructions:
Row 1: Work 1-sc, ch-3 62 times on each side, while making it once at each corner. End with ch-2 and make a loop with sc worked in sc on the previous row. **Row 2:** 2 loops of net st make 1 pattern. Repeat 2-dc together, ch-7. At corners, 3 loops of net st make 2 patterns. **Row 3:** Repeat ch-3, 1-sc, ch-5, 1-sc in loops on the previous row around.

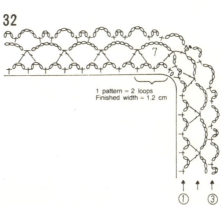

1 pattern = 2 loops
Finished width = 1.2 cm

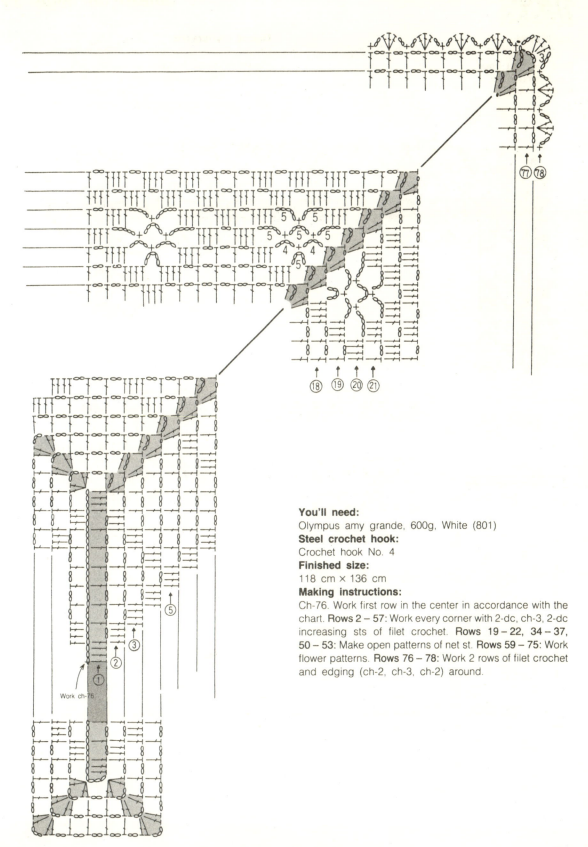

You'll need:
Olympus amy grande, 600g, White (801)
Steel crochet hook:
Crochet hook No. 4
Finished size:
118 cm × 136 cm
Making instructions:
Ch-76. Work first row in the center in accordance with the chart. **Rows 2 – 57:** Work every corner with 2-dc, ch-3, 2-dc increasing sts of filet crochet. **Rows 19 – 22, 34 – 37, 50 – 53:** Make open patterns of net st. **Rows 59 – 75:** Work flower patterns. **Rows 76 – 78:** Work 2 rows of filet crochet and edging (ch-2, ch-3, ch-2) around.

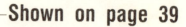

You'll need:
Crochet cotton DMC No. 40, 60g White (801)
Steel crochet hook:
Crochet hook No. I
Finished size:
33 cm × 70 cm

Making instructions:
Ch-157. Referring to the chart on measurement, work 112 rows of A – D patterns without any decrease or increase of sts. Work 3 rows of edging. 30 sts and (10 square meshes) 10 rows make 1 unit of A – D patterns. Size of a pattern differs depending on the type of pattern. Iron them to make all widths equal.

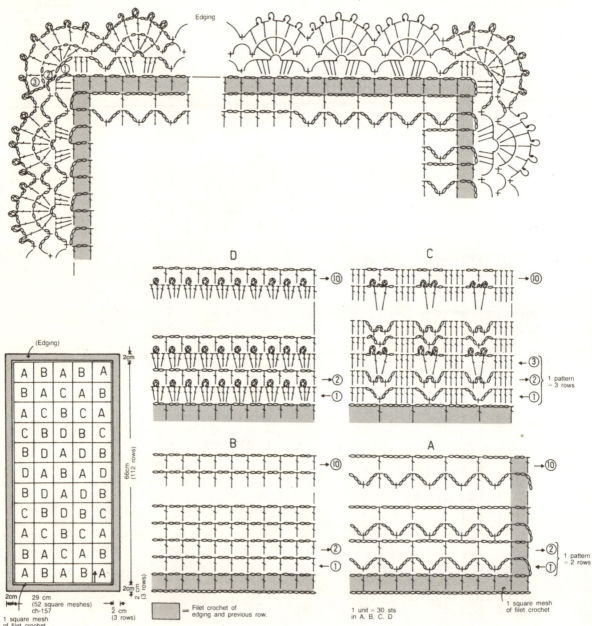

(Edging)

A	B	A	B	A
B	A	C	A	B
A	C	B	C	A
C	B	D	B	C
B	D	A	D	B
D	A	B	A	D
B	D	A	D	B
C	B	D	B	C
A	C	B	C	A
B	A	C	A	B
A	B	A	B	A

66cm (112 rows)

2cm

2cm (3 rows)
2 cm

2cm
29 cm (52 square meshes) ch-157

1 square mesh of filet crochet

2 cm (3 rows)

□ = Filet crochet of edging and previous row.

1 unit = 30 sts in A, B, C, D

1 square mesh of filet crochet

1 pattern = 3 rows

1 pattern = 2 rows

You'll need:
Crochet cotton DMC No. 40, 100g, White (801)
Brown inner-case satin cloth 82 cm by 41 cm, 300g kapok.

Steel crochet hook:
Crochet hook No. 4

Finished size of motif:
7.5 cm × 7.5 cm

Making instructions:
Ch-6, sl st in 1st ch to form a ring. **Row 1:** Ch-3, 15-dc in ring, sl st in 3rd st of beginning ch. **Row 2:** Repeat 4-ch, ch-7 4 times. **Row 3:** Work 4-dc together in each dc sts on the previous row and ch-5. Work 1-dc, ch-5, 1-dc at each corner. Work dc in st on the previous row. **Row 4:** Work one 3-dc-puff, ch-5 5 times in each corner to join 50 pieces of square motif. Leave opening for stuffing. Insert a inner-case (refer to p41 for making instructions) and stitch the opening closed.

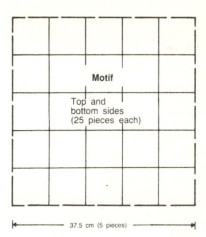

Motif

Top and
bottom sides
(25 pieces each)

◄──── 37.5 cm (5 pieces) ────►

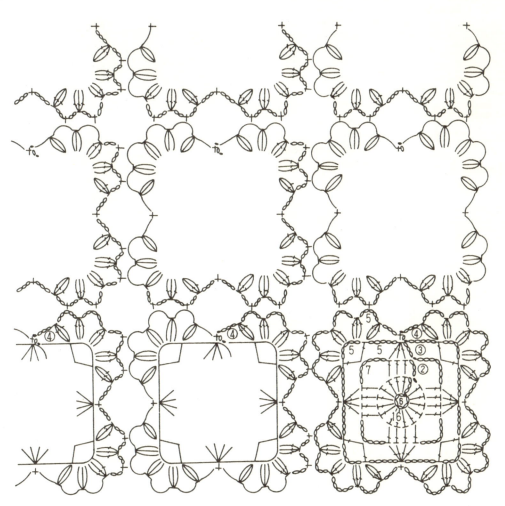

You'll need:
Crochet cotton DMC No. 40, 10g Bright green (261)
Steel crochet hook:
Crochet hook No. 4
Finished size:
5 cm in bottom diameter
5 cm in depth
Making instructions:
Ch-7, sl st in 1st ch to form a ring. **Row 1:** Ch-3, 17-dc in ring, sl st in 3rd st of beginning ch. **Row 2:** Ch-4 (1-dc, ch-1) 17 times. **Row 3:** Work 2-dc in each st on the previous row. **Row 4:** Work dc increasing sts in every third st. **Row 5:** Without decrease or increase in sts, work dc only for side of st on the previous row. **Row 6:** Ch-1, repeat 1-sc, ch-10, 6-dc from 5-sts behind, skip 3-dc on Row 5, 1-sc 18 times. **Row 7:** Referring to the chart, twist fabric clockwise and work 4-sc in ch around (72 sts in total). **Row 8:** Work the same as Row 6. **Rows 9 – 11:** Work sc same as Row 7. In Row 11 work 3-ch-p (sl st at the end p). Work 2-sc and 3-ch-p (sl st at the end p) between Row 4 and Row 5.

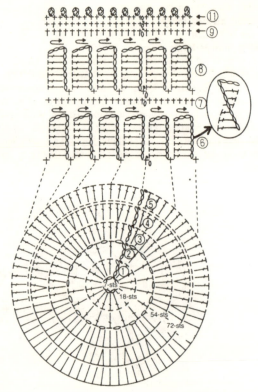

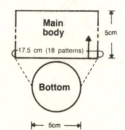

Main body

17.5 cm (18 patterns)

5cm

Bottom

5cm

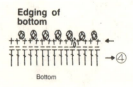

Edging of bottom

Bottom

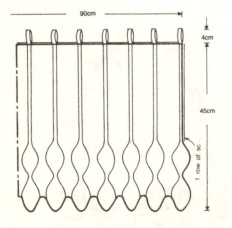

90cm

4cm

45cm

1 row of sc

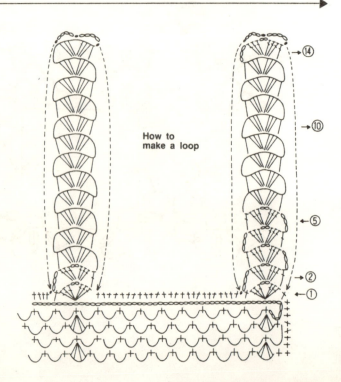

How to make a loop

55

You'll need:
Crochet cotton DMC No. 40, 120g White (801)
Steel crochet hook:
Crochet hook No. I
Finished size:
45 cm × 90 cm
Making instructions:
Ch-475. **Row 1:** Work net st of ch-5. **Row 2:** Repeat 1 shell st, 8 net sts. **Rows 3 – 60:** Work same as Row 1 and Row 2 alternatively. **Rows 61 – 92:** Work pineapple patterns in accordance with the chart. From Row 87, work a whole pattern one at a time.

Instructions for loop — **Row 1:** Join thread in. Work 1-sc and shell st of 3-dc, ch-2, 3-dc. Join to a main body with sc. Work until Row 14 in the same manner. Turn it down to the bottom side and work sl st of the beginning of sc. Work ch-4, sl st at the foot of shell st, ch-4 and work sl st in sc at the end of shell st. Work 1 row of sc until the next loop.

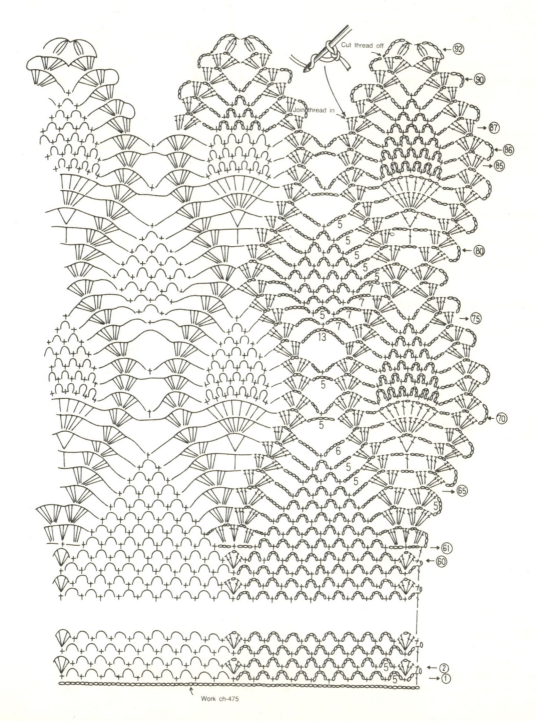

Work ch-475

Finishing

It is said that crochet work depends on its finishing. Finishing *is* very important. Crochet lace should always maintain its orderly stitches and beauty of pattern. Note the following points for an excellent finish.

Points to be checked before finishing
(1) Treatment of cotton ends before and after working. (2) Treatment of cotton ends which are connected or joined during working. (3) Checking for stains or spots on lace.

Tools required for finishing
(1) Ironing board (It should be soft and well padded to protect stitches). (2) Iron (3) Towel (4) Covering cloth [(3) and (4) should be plain white] (5) Detergent (neutral detergent) (6) Spray starch (7) Water sprayer (8) Finishing pins for handcraft (rust-proof) (9) Finishing board (e.g., sulfate paper, etc.)

Finished size
The sizes indicated in the directions are those after finishing. Therefore, the crocheted size is smaller than the finished size.

How to draw guide lines

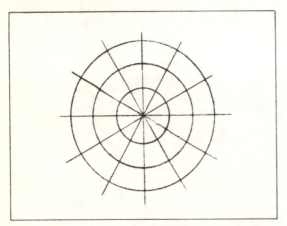

To the case of a circle, draw the circle to the finished size. Then, draw division lines according to the size of the pattern. (Draw with a fine line pen or a pencil.) In the case of

a pencil, iron on the drawing to avoid rise of lead. In the case of other shapes, draw lines according to a work, and follow the same procedure as for the circle.

How to pin

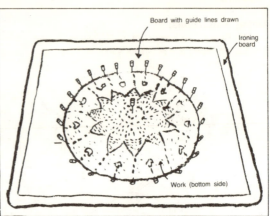

Turn over a work on a board. Pin at the center first. Then, pin at appropriate places according to the guide lines and the stretching capacity of the crochet. Increase the number of pins gradually. When a piece is well-stretched, remove the pin at the center before ironing.

How to iron

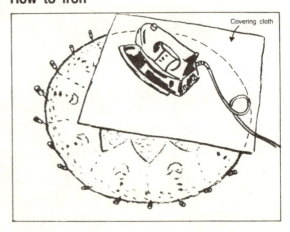

After water is sprayed all over the crochet, spray starch. Iron it, very hot, over a covering cloth. Be careful not to burn the crochet. After it is dried completely, remove pins. (Stains or spots on lace should be washed out beforehand.)

Index

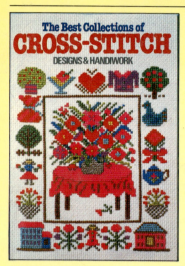

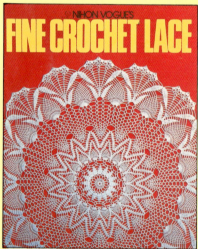